Teaching Reading as a Language Experience
Third Edition

Teaching Reading as a Language Experience
Third Edition

MaryAnne Hall
Georgia State University

Charles E. Merrill Publishing Company
A Bell & Howell Company
Columbus   Toronto   London   Sydney

Published by Charles E. Merrill Publishing Company
A Bell & Howell Company
Columbus, Ohio 43216

This book was set in Optima, Peignot
Production Editor: Kathy Vance Gillis
Cover Design Coordination: Will Chenoweth
Cover Photo: Alan Bass
Photo Credits: Dan Unkefer, p. 113; all other photographs by Wes Wright.

Library of Congress Catalog Number: 80–82458
International Standard Book Number: 0–675–08080–0
Printed in the United States of America

1 2 3 4 5 6 7 8 9 10—85 84 83 82 81

Contents

Preface

The purpose of this book, as stated in the preface to the first edition, is "to describe this approach and to identify instructional practices that can be followed in teaching reading in the language experience approach." The intent is to again provide guidance for the teacher who wants to use a language experience program for teaching reading and the other language arts. Guidance for the teacher consists not only of ideas and procedures for classroom activities but also explanations that clarify how these ideas and procedures relate to the nature of language learning and teaching.

The major difference between the first and second editions was the expansion of the theoretical foundations of language experience communication and the extension of instructional suggestions. The section on prereading was also expanded so as to give greater attention to language experience activities prior to beginning reading. Those emphases are maintained in this third edition. The major differences here are in the revision of the chapter on written expression and the addition of a chapter on comprehension. These changes were essential in order to reflect the new research in reading comprehension and on the writing process. The changes were also necessary to reflect my views of language experience learning as a means of acquiring literacy. Understanding in reading and effective communication through writing are central to language experience programs, and the new chapters on comprehension and writing reflect both the receptive and productive dimensions of the communication and their interrelatedness.

Since the time of the publication of the previous editions, I have visited a number of reading and language arts programs throughout the country and consulted with a number of regular classroom teachers, as well as teachers in specially funded local and state programs. Repeatedly, I would find teachers committed to and implementing language experience learning, and also repeatedly I would find those who had never tried a language based program. Although some concerns among teachers and administrators would be unique for a particular local system, many of the concerns and questions were the same regardless of the geographic location or previous exposure to language experience programs. In this edition, I have tried to address some of the universal concerns about implementation, about interpretation to parents and the general public, and about the day-to-day teaching of reading.

The revisions to both the second and third editions stem from extensive contact with children and teachers in schools throughout the country. Again and again, the same questions would occur among a group of teachers trying language experience techniques for the first time. One common reaction is what I call the doubting one—"Can an idea so seemingly simple be trusted in the implementation of a reading program?" I'm reminded of Eric Hoffer's statement, "It is not at all simple to understand the simple." Another reaction is that of "It sounds like too much work." To that my response is for those who are willing—as good teachers are—there are different ways of expending effort in teaching reading. "Too much work" may be related to "I'm not sure how to do it." Another reaction of teachers is "It makes so much sense." Of course, these perceptive teachers are the ones that save a consultant's day! Hopefully, in practice, the sensible grasp of what constitutes effective reading instruction can be combined with a knowledge of how to implement language experience reading programs.

As noted in the preface to the first edition, the book is *not* a collection of practices for teaching. However, ideas for teaching are presented as illustrations of the language experience approach in action. This book *is* a description of the theoretical base of the language experience approach and the implementation of this theoretical base in a classroom setting. The practical ideas included are to illustrate the basic philosophy of fostering communication in a creative, personal, and functional way of learning and teaching.

I believe that communication fluency can best be developed in an integrated and functional framework of teaching reading and language skills. Integrating reading instruction with the other language arts has long been a goal of reading programs, and the language experience approach truly illustrates this goal through all classroom reading experiences. Another belief is that teachers should recognize the linguistic nature of the reading process and adapt instructional practices for teaching reading with an emphasis on communication.

The book is organized in two parts. The first two chapters establish the theoretical background of the language experience approach and its relationship to the total elementary reading and language curriculum. The last eight chapters are concerned with the practical implementation of the language experience approach in the classroom. These chapters discuss experience stories, creative written expression, comprehension, vocabulary development, and literature experiences as well as the teaching of specific prereading and word analysis strategies. The final chapter summarizes the information presented and describes an effective setting for the language experience approach.

While this book is devoted exclusively to language experience reading, the reader should not assume that this approach is advocated by me as the only means for teaching reading or that this approach is without limitations. Informed teachers will utilize practices from a variety of approaches. This source can add to the background of the elementary teacher who wishes to draw upon the language experience framework as one component in a total reading program.

I also want to encourage and support those insightful and gifted teachers who continue to believe in and to practice true communication-

---

Eric Hoffer, *The Passionate State of Mind* (New York: Harper and Row, Publishers, 1955, 1968), p. 125.

centered learning through the rich immersion in language-rich environments, despite the all too oppressive pressures that mitigate against learning that is not directly prescribed and predetermined by a set of materials.

Special thanks go to the many teachers and teacher education students who tried and revised some of the procedures described here. Their comments greatly clarified the activities. Special thanks go also to Wes Wright who was the photographer and to Mary Jean Ligon for her help with the arrangements for the photographs in Nancy Creek Elementary School in DeKalb County, Georgia. As usual, Virginia Wolfe was my competent typist and Del Cardwell, my understanding and indespensible secretary.

1

THE NATURE of THE LANGUAGE EXPERIENCE APPROACH

The essence of the language experience approach is the use of the language and thinking of the learner as a foundation for reading instruction. Each learner's language and personal experiences are used to create reading materials that help show the reader the relationship between written language and his already familiar oral language. This chapter expands upon the preceding explanation and explores the linguistic and psychological foundations of this approach.

A DESCRIPTION of THE APPROACH

The cornerstones of language experience learning are language and experience and the interrelatedness of the two. Loban comments on the importance of these learning components, "Through experience and through language we learn. Experience needs language to give it form. Language needs experience to give it content."[1] The form and content of language experience reading programs are the language and experiences of the learner, and the form and content will differ from child to child and from group to group.

Sylvia Ashton-Warner has written movingly of the power of language experience learning in *Teacher.*[2] She says, "I reach a hand into the mind of a child, bring out a handful of the stuff I find there, and use that as our first working material. Whether it is good or bad stuff, violent or placid stuff, coloured or dun."[3] In another book, *Spearpoint,* she expresses the heart of language experience: "The professional formula—Release the native imagery of our child and use it for working material—remains timeless, changeless and axiomatic, but the application of it needs constant variation."[4]

The language experience approach for teaching reading is based on the interrelatedness of language and reading with the experience of the learner as the core from which language communication radiates. Language experience reading is viewed as a communication process closely related to communication in speaking, listening, and writing. The approach uses children's oral language and experiences for the creation of personal reading materials. This approach to reading integrates the teaching of reading with the other language arts as children listen, speak, write, and read about their personal experiences and ideas. A child's speech determines the *language patterns* of the reading materials, and his experiences determine the *content.* The language experience approach is based on the concept that reading has the most meaning to a pupil when the materials being read are expressed in his language and are rooted in his experiences.

As children see their spoken thoughts put into written form, they can grasp the concept that communication is the purpose of reading. Communication is stressed as children speak, see the speech represented by printed symbols, and then read the written representation of their speech. The association of meaning with the print is built into the reading of the personally created materials of the language experience approach. As the child sees his speech encoded into the printed symbols, he is aware of communicating through writing. As he reads or listens to the written representation of his thoughts, he is communicating through reading.

Reading is not "talk written down," but instead is the process of comprehending a message from print. In the language experience approach, the written record itself may be viewed as "talk written down," but the reading of the written record involves processing the printed symbols to arrive at a meaningful interpretation. Without meaning, it is not reading. According to one first grader, "Reading is saying the words. You have to say them right." However, reading should be the process of getting meaning from print. *Language experience reading is meaning-centered.*

CHARACTERISTICS

The characteristics of the language experience approach were implied in the preceding description, but for purposes of emphasis, the major characteristics are highlighted.

Use of Whole Language

Language experience reading is based on the use of whole language. The units of language in language experience reading and writing are sentence and story units. As children's talk is used to create materials, sentences and stories will naturally be used. There is no attempt to simplify the language samples by altering sentence structure or controlling either the vocabulary or sentence patterns. As explained on page 8, whole language is necessary in order to use the three cue systems, the graphophonic, the semantic, and the syntactic. Even the prereaders, the beginners, and the remedial readers will be presented with whole language in language experience programs. There is not meaningful language without use of the three cue systems. The focus is on units of communication, not isolated fragments, as is often found in programs with great stress on individual words and on isolated sound-letter correspondence learning.

Pupil-composed Materials

Pupil-composed materials constitute a major source of reading materials in the language experience approach. Reading materials are developed as children talk about their ideas and experiences; their talk is recorded, and the written record is then used for reading. In initial reading instruction, group and individual experience stories are used for reading instruction instead of published reading materials. Although pupil-produced materials are of prime importance, other materials also are utilized since children need to develop proficiency in reading and obtaining meaning from many types of materials. As children advance, supplementary reading of selections from basal readers, trade books, newspapers, content area texts, and other materials is included in a well-rounded reading program. Chapters 3–9 devote considerable attention to the various types of and procedures for using pupil-developed reading materials.

Interrelationship

The interrelationship of all the communication skills is stressed. Reading is not taught apart from but is dependent upon and integrated with the other facets of the language arts. Reading is a language activity, and the ability to communicate through language is essential for success in reading. The four facets of the language arts can be classified as either receptive or expressive. Listening and reading are receptive, while speaking and writing are expressive. In the language experience approach, children's listening, speaking, and writing are incorporated with reading instruction. As children increase their listening and speaking facility, they increase their ability to understand

3

ideas encountered in their reading. Writing particularly is tied to reading in that both of these processes deal with written language.

No Vocabulary Controls

There are no vocabulary controls in the reading materials other than the extent of a child's speaking vocabulary. The initial reading material is not limited to a few simple words or to short, artificial sentence patterns with a planned amount of repetition. There is, however, the inescapable repetition of frequently used words. In recording the pupil's speech, the teacher should *not* shorten or alter sentences in an attempt to control vocabulary. In the language experience approach when a pupil reads content that he has first spoken, the teacher is certain that the words and syntactical patterns employed in reading are comprehensible to him and that they are part of his existing language repertoire. Ways of developing both speaking and reading vocabularies are discussed in chapter 5.

Attributes of the Approach

Definitions and characteristics provide one means of describing the language experience approach. However, teachers who work with this approach need a greater understanding of the philosophical framework or the distinctive attributes than that supplied by the definition and explanation given for the characteristics. The language experience approach is a personal, communicative, creative, and purposeful way of learning and teaching.

Personal

The language experience approach is a personal way of learning and teaching. Language experience reading starts with and values the reader—his thoughts, his experiences, his language, his products, his uniqueness. The language experience rationale and the application of the approach can be appropriate for many, but in each case the person makes the language experience materials unique. Language experience reading is free and unstandardized. The learner in the language experience approach is actively involved in the reading process as he creates and shares his reading. In the language experience approach it is possible to have material of high personal interest to each child. Group writing experiences are encouraged, but since the content of group stories will be related to common experiences and group interests, these materials will also be personal to the group members.

All teachers are confronted daily with the problem of creating an instructional program designed to reach individual interests and levels. Pupil-composed materials are one means of personalizing reading instruction. Robert Frost is reported to have said that the materials that help a good mind achieve the freedom essential for creativity are always different for each person.[5] The language experience approach uses different personal materials for each student.

COMMUNICATIVE

The language experience approach is a communicative way of learning and teaching. In the language experience approach, reading occurs in a communication context, and words are introduced, not in isolation, but in conjunction with the expression of thought. The child realizes that the printed words and sentences are a representation of an event or thought he already understands or has experienced. Dechant comments on the role of communication in reading:

> Communication is the heart of the language arts. Without communication listening or reading cannot occur. Reading takes place only when the child shares the ideas that the communicator intends to convey.[6]

In the language experience approach the child communicates personally through the medium of print.

Communication requires effective use of language, and it is a goal of the language experience approach to develop children's language power by providing a rich language environment and the opportunity to articulate their thoughts. Allen refers to raising a child's level of sensitivity to his environment and heightening his awareness of language as a means of expressing his knowledge of his world.[7] Directed language study starts at the present level of language development of the learner. In order to promote communication, the teacher must accept the language of the children and not block their speech through an emphasis on correction in the early stages of reading instruction. Also to be encouraged is experimentation in writing since such experimentation is often very motivating to young children.

CREATIVE

The language experience approach is a creative way of learning and teaching. Creative thinking is an essential component in this approach to learning since children conceptualize thoughts and feelings through spoken and written language. Divergent responses are encouraged, accepted, and valued as children express themselves. Therefore, by using the child's created materials for reading, creative thinking becomes a natural part of the learning act.

Teachers who encourage creativity in pupils realize that the classroom environment must stimulate inventive thinking. The elementary school years are critical in the development of creative talent. Wilt comments on the teacher's role in freeing children to create: "First, you must believe that if a child is really to create something it must grow out of frequent opportunities to experiment and grope for his own best way to express his idea."[8] Teachers who use the language experience approach must believe

5

that each child has some potential for creating and that he can express his efforts through language.

These children are experiencing another student's creative story as dictated to the teacher.

In classrooms where children's stories and language are accepted and valued, further expression is facilitated. A perfect final product is not the goal as much as the *process* of creating and communicating through spoken and written language. The teacher's responsibility is to stimulate originality. In order for children to create through language, they must hear creative language models of others and use language creatively in their own expression of ideas.

Purposeful

The language experience approach is a purposeful way of learning and teaching. The role of purpose in learning is well established by learning theorists and educators. In the language experience approach, learning is purposeful when pupils feel a need to communicate through language activities. Language experience reading starts with and values communication. To communicate is the reason to read and to write. The language experience learner views reading and writing as tools and processes for communication. Having important things to say, to read, and to write will be necessary for language experience learning. When a child has a personal stake in or purpose for learning to read, that purpose can have positive effects on his learning.

The language experience approach stresses the role of functional reading very early in the total reading program. Functional reading, which uses reading as a tool for learning as distinguished from learning the skills for "how to read," constitutes one of the major aspects of a comprehensive reading program. In many school programs, functional reading does not receive much emphasis until the intermediate grades. However, functional reading is incorporated into the language experience approach in the beginning stages since the production of reading materials is often an outgrowth of classroom activities in content areas such as science and social studies. Real world materials such as menus, signs, labels, and directions for toys and games can also provide functional reading situations for children, and children often enjoy composing their own "real world" materials for classroom projects, displays, and activities. Significant class activities maintain interest and motivation at a high level.

Linguistic Foundations

There is a strong linguistic rationale for teaching reading with the language experience approach. The linguistic foundations for language experience reading are related to the view that reading is a language-based process, that the nature of language as a communication system has implications for the teaching of reading as a form of language communication, that readers— even beginners and remedial students—are users of language, and that the interrelationship of oral and written language affects the reading process. Since reading is communication through written language, all reading is linguistic. However, language experience reading, more than other instructional methods, offers instruction which makes it possible to capitalize on the relationship of oral and written language.

Language-Based Process

Reading is a language-based process, dependent upon the processing of meaning through the use of printed symbols. Definitions of reading are numerous and vary according to the degree of emphasis placed on the recognition of symbols and the importance of meaning. The definition of reading intended in this book is that of Goodman's explanation of the reading process as "the reconstruction of a message from print."[9] Meaning is an essential component in this definition. Regardless of materials and methodology employed in teaching reading, a reader must be able to process the information represented by the print. Language experience reading does not change the process of reading; however, it does make it possible for the process to be more natural for the beginner.

Symbol System

Language as a symbol system for communication affects the teaching of reading in the approach as communication through printed language symbols. Goodman comments, "If the written language children encounter right from the beginning is whole, real, natural, and relevant, they will be able to use their existing language competence as they learn to read."[10] Reading is an interaction of the reader's language and thought with the author's language and thought. If the reader is also the author, the beginning reading task can be made easier than when the beginner is required to read unfamiliar language. To learn language, individuals must learn a code; and fortunately, when most children begin to learn the written code, they already possess knowledge of the oral code. Of course, deaf children are an exception in this respect. However, written language for the deaf can still use language experience by relating print to signing (if they have learned signing) and/or by starting with written language that represents content of importance to them.[11]

Language is systematic and patterned. The language system includes phonology, or the sound system, as well as the orthography, the written system of a language. In acquiring literacy, learners must acquire knowledge of the relationships between the phonology and the orthography of the language. In addition to the phonological system of language, there is also the system of meaning. The semantic information of a language and the syntax, or grammatical patterning, of language affect a reader's ability to read with meaning. Goodman has described the three categories of language information as:

1. *Graphophonic.* This is the information from the writing system and from the phonological system of oral language. Phonics is the name generally used when discussing the teaching of the code system of letter-sound relationships.
2. *Syntactic Information.* This is the information from grammatical structures of the language. The language user knows syntactical or sentence patterns and, therefore, is able to use this information orally before he learns to read his native language.
3. *Semantic Information.* This is information related to meaning and concepts represented by the printed words.[12]

User of Language

Also basic to the linguistic foundations for the language experience approach is the concept that every reader, even the beginner, is a user of language. The language and experience five- and six-year-old children bring to school provide a foundation for reading instruction. The child who comes to kindergarten and first grade not yet knowing how to read does know his native language. The remedial student who has failed at reading also knows the oral language system. The language learning of the preschool year is extensive, and the school beginner possesses considerable linguistic performance and competence. The existing language of the beginning reader is a foundation upon which reading instruction is built.

Language use is both receptive and productive. The preschool child learns to be both a producer and a receiver as he participates in communication situations orally as a listener and as a speaker. In the school situation he must learn two additional communication processes—one receptive and one productive—as he learns to receive printed messages in reading and to produce or encode messages in writing.

Children learn oral language as they use language functionally. Halliday, a British linguist, has explored children's oral learning from the standpoint of the functions of language determining the learning of that language.[13] The learning of written language through realistic use may make the learning of written language more natural and more effective than is often true when traditional materials that are not at all related to real communication—thus, not perceived by children as functional and thus sometimes ineffective in learning—are used.

For the beginning reader, the teaching of reading should focus on helping him to make the connection between spoken and written language. The natural language of the reading material created by children in the language experience approach provides an excellent vehicle for demonstrating that language conveys meaning and for showing that the written code represents the oral code. Stauffer maintains, ". . . reading is one facet of language and one means of communication and should from the very beginning of reading instruction be taught as such through a language-experience approach."[14]

Facility in oral language is one important foundation for success in reading. Research confirms that children's achievement in oral and written language is related. Ruddell states:

> The research and opinion would suggest that an instructional program
> designed to develop an understanding of the relationship between
> the child's familiar spoken system of communication and written
> language would facilitate his ability to comprehend written
> material.[15]

Although the oral and written codes of language are closely related, they are not the same. Speech is the primary form of language; writing is a secondary symbol system and is an imperfect representation of speech. While the language experience reading material represents children's "talk written down," the process of reading is that of reconstructing a message from print. Smith maintains that the understanding that spoken and written language are different is an essential one for the beginning reader, and he chides some proponents of language experience programs for conveying the erroneous idea that the spoken and written language are the same.[16] The abstractness of written language is thought to be a stumbling block to the

9

acquisition of literacy skills. Language experience reading can lessen the abstractness of written language by using material of high comprehensibility.

In an integrated approach to teaching communication skills, the existing linguistic performance and competence are in understanding and using oral language function as the starting point for developing competence in reading and writing. Teachers need to be cognizant of the interrelatedness of oral and written language and to capitalize on this interrelatedness as they teach children to communicate effectively in reading, speaking, listening, and writing.

Psychological Foundations

Since many of the psychological underpinnings of language experience learning were noted in the section on attributes, the following discussion only highlights certain psychological foundations for the language experience approach. Psychologically, the factors of success, motivation, interest, and attitude, which affect self-concept and achievement, support the use of the language experience approach. The setting and material for language experience activities should maximize favorable conditions for learning. The language experience approach fosters success along with a favorable attitude toward reading and the self. Through successful experiences in language experience activities and through the individually created materials, a healthy self-image can be promoted. The motivation to read generated by the stories and books produced by children is maintained through the pride of authorship and through the recognition that comes from classroom displays and sharing of those productions.

Language experience learning has a humanistic quality shown by the respect and acceptance of the learner as he is. This respect and acceptance means respect and acceptance for the experience, the thinking, the culture, and the language that the learner brings with him to the school setting. The humanistic quality of the language experience approach is also demonstrated by the belief that the learner can participate in determining the substance of his learning.

Summary

The unique feature of the language experience approach is the use of reading materials created by the learner about his experiences and expressed in his language patterns. The teaching of reading in the language experience approach is integrated with the other communication skills in an instructional framework that stresses the personal, communicative, creative, and purposeful nature of this approach. Learning written language is related to the oral language learning already acquired.

The linguistic base for the language experience approach rests upon a definition of reading as the processing of written language and upon a view of the reader as a user of language. The psychological base of the approach rests upon a view of the actively involved learner and on the powerful and favorable effect of successful language experience learning on interest, attitude, motivation, and self-concept.

Notes

1. Walter Loban, "What Language Reveals," in *Language and Meaning,* ed. James B. Macdonald and Robert R. Leeper (Washington, D.C.: Association for Supervision and Curriculum Development, 1966), p. 73.
2. Sylvia Ashton-Warner, *Teacher* (New York: Simon and Schuster, 1963).
3. Ashton-Warner, *Teacher,* p. 34.
4. Sylvia Ashton-Warner, *Spearpoint* (New York: Alfred A. Knopf, 1972), p. 17.
5. Sidney Cox, *A Swinger of Birches: A Portrait of Robert Frost* (New York: Collier Books, 1961), p. 53.
6. Emerald V. Dechant, *Improving the Teaching of Reading,* 2d ed. (Englewood Cliffs, N.J.: Prentice-Hall, 1970), p. 111.
7. Roach V. Allen, *Attitudes and the Art of Teaching Reading* (Washington, D.C.: National Education Association, 1965), pp. 3–12.
8. Miriam E. Wilt, *Creativity in the Elementary School* (New York: Appleton-Century-Crofts, 1959), p. 8.
9. Kenneth S. Goodman, ed., *The Psycholinguistic Nature of the Reading Process* (Detroit: Wayne State University Press, 1968), p. 15.
10. Kenneth S. Goodman, "Miscues: Windows on the Reading Process," in *Miscue Analysis,* ed. Kenneth S. Goodman (Urbana, Ill.: ERIC Clearinghouse on Reading and Communication Skills, 1973). p. 13.
11. Russell G. Stauffer, "The Language Experience Approach to Reading Instruction for Deaf and Hearing Impaired Children," *The Reading Teacher* 33 (October 1979): 21–24.
12. Kenneth S. Goodman, "Analysis of Oral Reading Miscues: Applied Psycholinguistics," *Reading Research Quarterly* 5 (Fall 1969): 17–18.
13. Michael A. K. Halliday, *Explorations in the Functions of Language* (London: Edward Arnold, 1973).
14. Russell G. Stauffer, "Certain Convictions about Reading Instruction," *Elementary English* 46 (January 1969): 86.
15. Robert B. Ruddell, "Reading Instruction in First Grade with Varying Emphasis on the Regularity of Grapheme-Phoneme Correspondences and the Relation of Language Structure to Meaning—Extended into Second Grade," *The Reading Teacher* 20 (May 1967): 731.
16. Frank Smith, "Making Sense of Reading and Reading Instruction," *Harvard Educational Review* 47 (August 1977): 386–395.

Suggested Readings

ALLEN, ROACH V. *Language Experiences in Communication.* Boston: Houghton Mifflin, 1976. Allen offers considerable detail on language experience learning in the elementary curriculum in communication skills. The first four chapters are an overview of language experience considerations, and the remaining chapters describe the implementation of language experience activities.

ASHTON-WARNER, SYLVIA. *Teacher.* New York: Simon & Schuster, 1963. A personal account of Mrs. Ashton-Warner's experiences teaching Maori children in New Zealand, this book presents an inspiring philosophy of the language experience approach.

BRAUN, CARL, AND FROESE, VICTOR, eds. *An Experience Based Approach to Language and Reading.* Baltimore: University Park Press, 1977. This volume is one which contains considerable treatment of the rationale for language experience learning as well as consideration of language experience in conjunction with content areas, composition, poetry, diagnostic teaching, and evaluation.

CRAMER, RONALD L. *Writing, Reading, and Language Growth.* Columbus, Ohio: Charles E. Merrill, 1978. Cramer's presentation of language learning and teaching is one that values creative personal expression in both reading and writing. Chapter 3 is devoted to explanation of the language experience approach.

HALL, MARYANNE. "Language-Centered Reading: Premises and Recommendations," *Language Arts* 56 (September 1979): 664–670. The nature of reading as a language-based process is the topic of this article. The view of the article is also the view of language experience reading presented in this text.

————."Linguistically Speaking, Why Language Experience," *The Reading Teacher* 25 (January 1972): 328–31. Linguistic reasons for using the language experience approach for beginning readers are presented.

HALL, MARYANNE, and RAMIG, CHRISTOPHER J. *Linguistic Foundations of Reading.* Columbus, Ohio: Charles E. Merrill, 1978. This textbook explores the linguistic nature of the reading process as well as discussing the implications of the language base for classroom instruction in reading.

LEE, DORRIS M., and ALLEN, R. V. *Learning to Read through Experience.* New York: Appleton-Century-Crofts, 1963. The first chapter of Lee and Allen's book stresses the interrelatedness of the communication skills and elaborates a child's concept of reading in a language experience framework.

STAUFFER, RUSSELL G. *The Language Experience Approach to the Teaching of Reading.* New York: Harper & Row, 1980. Dr. Stauffer presents a thorough discussion of the philosophy and the implementation of language experience teaching.

2

The Language Experience Approach in the Total Reading Program

The language experience approach in the total school reading program can be studied from several perspectives. After a brief explanation of the evolvement of the approach, this chapter will examine it as an approach for prereading and initial reading instruction, a supplement to other approaches beyond the beginning stages, and an approach for remedial readers, culturally and linguistically different children, and adult illiterates.

This chapter also discusses how this approach relates to the goals of an elementary reading and language arts program. The remaining chapters suggest specific instruction towards these goals.

Evolvement of the Approach

The beginnings of the language experience approach can be traced to the old sentence and story methods popular in the middle of the nineteenth century and to the use of experience story material in the progressive education movement of the 1930s. Hildreth presents an excellent historical perspective on the evolution of the approach from its classroom origins around 1900 through the studies investigating the approach from 1926 to 1965.[1] She notes that the term *experience method* did not appear until 1934 and that the designation *language experience* was not used until considerably later.

After Sylvia Ashton-Warner wrote about her work in New Zealand, the result was new interest in the approach in the United States.[2] Language experience reading surfaced significantly with the work of Roach Van Allen in the San Diego, California schools in the late 1950s. The programs then spread across the United States.

Through the 1960s, instruction using this approach increased considerably. The National First Grade Studies, the largest research project ever in beginning reading, included it as one of the major approaches studied.[3] Language experience programs were employed from Delaware to New York, Texas to Colorado, and Pennsylvania to California.

In that decade the approach was validated on the basis of its mention in textbooks, at reading conferences, and in research studies. As interest in sociolinguistic and psycholinguistic study has grown, the theoretical rationale supporting the use of the program has become more extensive and convincing. The need for appropriate materials for the learners not of the mainstream culture has also supported the use of language experience reading. The informal, open education movement in British schools has also contributed to the acceptance of the setting that is conducive to language experience learning.

Since the beginning of the 1970s, language experience teaching has received more attention in methods textbooks than ever before, and more preservice and inservice teacher education has been devoted to this approach; therefore, more teachers than ever are equipped to implement these programs. In recent years, the concern about the quality of written expression at all academic levels has also helped to support these programs, which promote the development of competence in written expression. Another indication of support is *The Journal of Language Experience* (begun in the academic year 1978/79) which is published by the Language Experience Special Interest Group of the International Reading Association. The research support for the effectiveness of language experience programs also should lead to increased acceptance of such programs.

Research confirms this method's effectiveness in teaching beginning reading. In a review of thirteen research studies on the language experience approach from 1926 to 1965, Hildreth reports positive results for this approach in eleven instances.[4] When achievement scores in reading were compared in a study of the basal reader, individualized, and language experience approaches in San Diego County, California, the language experience approach was found to be as effective as the other two approaches in the primary grades.[5] In the National First Grade Studies, the language experience approach was found to be an effective means of teaching beginning reading.[6] One reason for the effectiveness of the approach was noted by Hahn. He comments that the time provided for purposeful writing, speaking, and listening in conjunction with wide reading contributed to the reading achievement of pupils using it.[7] In a 1978 publication, Hall reviews the research on language experience programs and reports favorable results for this approach on measures of reading achievement including comprehension and vocabulary, as well as favorable results on measures of spelling, creative writing, and creativity.[8] Stauffer reviews eighteen studies which focus on classroom application of language experience procedures and again favorable results are noted.[9]

Prereaders and Beginners

The major application of the language experience approach has been as a way of teaching prereading and beginning reading. The beginning reading stage is a crucial one since later attitudes and achievement are influenced by a child's progress and reactions to initial instruction. A child who experiences considerable frustration in beginning reading is very likely to develop a dislike of reading, which will be a barrier to his progress at later stages. The role of success in learning to read is extremely important. The language experience approach stresses success as the beginning reader is able to read his dictated stories since he is certain of the content of these stories.

As a child first learns to read, he learns to recognize printed symbols and to associate the print with meaning from his previous experiences. A child enters school with considerable competence in oral language, and the teaching of reading should be closely related to his present speech development. Before a child can comprehend the printed symbols of reading material, he must first be familiar with the oral language symbols and patterns that the printed words represent. The words and syntactical patterns a child encounters in beginning reading should be those which are already in his listening and speaking background. If the child has already learned the meaning of the words and is already familiar with the sentence patterns he sees in print, he can relate the printed symbols to concepts and language already known.

In addition to stressing the relationship of reading to speaking, the language experience approach relates reading to writing and provides children with the opportunity to write extensively. The report of the National First Grade Studies indicates that attention to writing experiences in conjunction with reading instruction is valuable. Dykstra notes that, "There is evidence that a writing component is an effective addition to a primary reading program."[10] Hildreth explains the advantages of correlating reading instruction with writing in the following statements:

Learning to read is reinforced by simultaneous experience in writing.

In writing familiar language patterns, the young writer creates material to read expanding the amount of reading material that it is easy

15

to understand because it reflects the child's own ideas, vocabulary, and modes of expression.

Writing furnishes practice in using words in meaningful sentences, strengthening the association between word forms and their meaning, and the child's familiarity with sentence patterns.[11]

Other evidence supporting early attention to writing comes from the investigations of reading prior to grade one. Durkin reported that children who learned to read early often expressed interest in lerning to write before expressing interest in reading and that writing often was a factor in learning to read.[12] Hall, Moretz, and Statom found that preschool children learned to write before learning to read and that the preschool children's writing was an effort to communicate.[13] Clay's work also provides a rationale for encouraging early writing, as she traces the acquisition of writing for preschoolers and beginning readers.[14] Language experience instruction can capitalize on writing as a tool of communication, and pupil authorship is begun early in language experience programs.

Many abilities are involved in learning to read. Initial instruction must include

1. Developing interest in reading
2. Building a reading vocabulary
3. Getting meaning from reading material
4. Developing strategies attacking unfamiliar words
5. Teaching left-to-right progression across a line of print

In both the prereading and initial reading stages, the students' facility in oral language and experience backgrounds should be broadened since understanding reading material is based on pupils' ability to understand oral language and on their experiences.

The language experience approach builds interest in reading through the pupils' personal involvement and motivation in creating their materials. A reading vocabulary is built, not through reading basal textbooks, but by recognizing words used in individual and class stories. Comprehension is present since the content is meaningful when first spoken. Some instruction in word analysis is begun as pupils notice the beginnings and endings of words and as they analyze some of the words in their word banks for similar phonic elements (see chapters 5 and 9). Children's attention is called to left-to-right progression in reading as the teacher reads the group experience stories aloud and helps children read their individual stories.

In beginning reading instruction, the pupil-composed materials include group and individual experience stories and group and individual word banks. A group experience story is a record of some common experience or topic interest that the pupils discuss and the teacher records. A personal story is told to the teacher who records or types it for the child's reading material. Individual word banks are built as a child identifies words in the the group experience stories and in his own stories. Words are written on separate cards or slips of paper to be kept by each child for his word bank. These banks can tell the teacher which words are in the child's reading vocabulary and can be used as examples for instruction in phonics. Group word banks can be compiled as the class studies different classifications of words. For example, there could be word categories of animals, colors, descriptions, and actions.

In beginning reading as well as at higher levels, a writing center is an important part of the classroom environment, and children's literature is a part of the total reading and language program. The writing center functions as a stimulus for independent creative writing and for following up language study as materials and ideas for creating stories are displayed. The literature experiences contribute to the motivation for reading and provide invaluable language enrichment.

Teaching reading begins by having a child dictate a story or by writing a group experience story with the total class. However, in the early stages of instruction, such instruction will have different emphases and values for different children. What is for some children a prereading experience is for other children a beginning reading activity. With the first stories some children will learn to read some words. Other children will be able to recognize likenesses and differences in printed words but will not be able to read individual words immediately. For some children the most important contribution the early stories can offer is helping them to see that their spoken ideas can be put into written form. Other children may profit most from the discussion that precedes the writing of the story. For all children the meaning of the written story should be clear.

When used as the major approach to beginning reading, the language experience approach can be used without systematic use of conventional instructional textbooks until pupils are reading at an advanced first grade level. At this level of reading development, this approach is used as a supplement to or in combination with reading textbooks or in a program of individualized reading in trade books.

Use with Other Approaches

In the total elementary reading program, the language experience approach has many advantages when used with other approaches. While teachers may not want to rely on this approach as the major means of reading instruction beyond the beginning stages, they will want to incorporate many of its aspects. The high degree of personal involvement and the functional application of reading, speaking, listening, and writing are features that strongly support the use of language experience beyond the initial reading stage. In fact, the activities suggested in chapters 3–10 can be easily incorporated into the language experience framework as a corollary to other approaches.

A number of authorities have commented on the value of an enriched reading program that combines features of various approaches.

One of the major findings of the National First Grade Studies is that any approach which is enriched with features of other approaches produces better reading achievement than the use of one approach exclusively.[15] Stauffer and Hammond report that the language experience approach, which was effective in grade one, continued to be effective at the second grade level.[16] They found that the pupils taught with this approach through the second grade develop better written communication than those taught with the basal reader approach. Kendrick and Bennett also found the language experience approach to be effective through the second grade.[17] Vilscek, Cleland, and Bilka note that pupils taught with the approach through the second grade could demonstrate superiority in comprehension of concepts and in reading in the content areas of science, social studies, and arithmetic. They felt that the diversity of reading probably contributed to this superiority.[18]

As children move beyond the initial stages of instruction, personally created reading materials have limitations for providing a complete reading program. While language experience materials offer sensible and relevant language, children will also need to read material that is not as completely predictable as their own productions. Other types of reading materials must be provided. Many of the enrichment suggestions in basal reader manuals can be combined with the ideas of the following chapters. The basal reading program can provide a systematic development of reading competence, while the language experience activities can add personal involvement and application of language learning.

Individualized reading which features the wide reading of library materials, pupil-teacher conferences, and self-selection can be combined with language experience activities. Some teachers who use the language experience approach in beginning reading move into an individualized program when children have acquired a sufficiently large reading vocabulary to read simple library books. The pupil-teacher conference is featured in the language experience method with the individual experience stories and in individualized reading discussions. Flexible grouping in the individualized program allows for formation of interest groups as children talk about their independent reading and as they share their personal stories with each other. The suggestions for working with literature in chapter 6 will be helpful in combining independent individualized reading with language experience activities.

Some teachers who are uncomfortable with language experience instruction for an entire class do believe in using it with certain students who have difficulty with or who reject the methods or materials being used with most children. One type of combined program, then, is to use this approach for some students while using different methods with other students. Teachers who are reluctant to teach reading with the language experience approach may use some of the language experience activities as part of the language arts curriculum, particularly in conjunction with other creative activities, for example, writing, literature, and drama.

18

Another possibility for combining language experience reading with the total curriculum is to use the creation of reading materials as a part of content area instruction. The purpose of listening, speaking, reading, and writing as tools for communication can be well demonstrated by functional use of these processes through projects that stress personal involvement and creative language use. The materials created can contribute to content area learning for all levels of students, and they can provide appropriate reading materials for poor readers since the content area texts are usually too advanced for the poor readers. Much content can be presented orally with children's interpretations recorded, and then the language experience procedures can be followed for reading instruction.

When the language experience approach is combined with other approaches, emphasis is placed on developing facility in written language, on enriching the speaking and writing vocabularies as well as the reading vocabulary, and on providing integration of reading with other facets of communication at the higher levels. The personal, communicative, creative, and purposeful attributes of this approach also operate when used with other approaches and materials. In a combined program beyond the primary grades, the pupil-composed materials are not used as much for reading as for stimulating creative expression, for developing power in communicating in spoken and written language, and for providing motivation for purposeful writing.

The contribution of language experience learning beyond the early stages is probably more to writing than to reading. Educators have probably done a better job of teaching reading than of teaching writing in the elementary schools. Many children (not to mention countless adults) who read quite well find writing clearly and expressively a difficult task. When many experiences in writing are offered in an experience framework along with the philosophy of creativity and acceptance, the hope is that students will learn to write effectively.

Remedial Readers

The language experience approach has merit for remedial readers who have experienced frustration in reading with conventional or traditional approaches. The psychological rationale for the language experience approach seems particularly significant for remedial readers. These children often exhibit a negative attitude toward reading and may reject remediation attempts that use more of the same type of instruction that was unsuccessful in the past. Attitude, success, and motivation are of primary importance in working with remedial readers. For pupils who possess a negative attitude toward reading as a result of repeated frustration and failure, the use of personally created materials can remove the fear of failure. The language experience approach promotes a favorable attitude toward reading and develops a high degree of personal involvement with intrinsic motivation as students experience success through the reading of their own stories.

Johnson states five fundamental principles of learning that underlie working with remedial readers:

1. Learning begins with the known.
2. Learning proceeds from concrete to abstract.
3. Learning demands active participation.
4. Learning should be goal directed.
5. Learning is an individual matter.[19]

The language experience approach does begin with known material which is easily decoded and understood, provides concrete materials as the starting point, actively involves the learner, helps the student set attainable goals, and promotes reading in an individual manner with concern for a personal involvement in the reading situation.

The linguistic rationale for the language experience approach also applies to remedial reading students. The view of reading as processing of ideas presented in written language should underlie remedial instruction. Often the remedial student has been given narrow and distorted reading instruction that has focused on small units of language and on isolated skills without a meaningful language base. Meaningful language contained in sentence and story units can help remedial students to use semantic and syntactic clues in reading as well as the clues contained in the graphophonic information.

The descriptions of the language experience approach and the techniques described in chapters 3–10 can be adapted for remedial reading instruction. The basic idea of starting with the pupil's language to create reading materials is again followed when this approach is used with remedial readers. Using the reader's spoken language is an advantage since the remedial student has usually advanced in oral language beyond the language of the textbooks on her instructional level. For example, the fifth grade child who is reading on a first grade reading level will be more advanced in her oral language than the language employed in a first grade reader, and she will have little interest in the content of a book designed for a child of six.

When using language experience reading with remedial readers, it is important to remember that although the procedures will be similar to those recommended for younger students, the content will be quite different. The principle of using the concerns of the students remains, but those concerns will differ considerably at different age levels. Subjects which appeal to older students are cars, motorcycles, sports, music, and entertainers. One teacher has reported successful results when using the advertising material from automobile agencies. Another has reported that the use of the explanatory material on favorite record albums of students was successful in motivating students to produce language experience materials. Sports pictures from magazines and newspapers can also lead to the creation of individual and group stories. Books students create about favorite sports or entertainment figures are usually popular reading materials. Spitzer reports that language experience reading has been miraculously effective for middle school remedial students in building both confidence and reading ability.[20] She starts with some students by having them paraphrase comic book stories, which she reads to them. She does not expect "word-perfect" reading but instead seeks to have students use the flow of language and the known meaning to help students realize that they *can read* and *are reading* for meaning.

Language experience for remedial students often serves as a bridge to basal readers, trade books, and other reading materials. After the student has experienced some success through his own stories, he can move on to other materials, or the language experience procedures can be integrated with a combined approach. As he works with experience stories, needed work in vocabulary and word analysis strategies can be provided by studying words used in his stories that illustrate the particular patterns to be mastered. Comprehension also can be developed through the personal experience stories especially if he has a tendency to "word-call" instead of reading with meaning. The obvious strength of language experience instruction for illustrating that reading is for the communication of meaning is one reason why it can be effective with students who have viewed reading as word-calling.

Obviously, teachers should carefully evaluate each remedial reader's strengths and weaknesses and adapt the instructional approach to the particular reading needs of each student. Specific strengths and deficiencies must be diagnosed and appropriate instruction offered. This approach is not a panacea for all remedial cases, but it may help some children with reading difficulties gain confidence and a realization of the relationship between oral and written language.

Culturally and Linguistically Different Children

The language experience approach seems particularly appropriate for use with children whose language patterns and life experiences differ considerably from the language and content of many commercial reading materials, since language experience teaching makes it possible to have materials that match both the experiences and language patterns of the learners.

Typically, many children not of the mainstream culture experience considerable difficulty and frustration with traditional methods of reading instruction. As a result of reading problems, these children are handicapped in all school activities that require reading. The language experience approach for culturally and linguistically divergent children is of greatest relevance in the beginning stages of instruction; however, it continues to be important for teaching communication at higher levels.

A number of factors can be cited for the difficulties some culturally and linguistically different children experience in reading. Among those factors are lack of readiness for school, limited and/or different experience backgrounds, use of language patterns that may differ from "school language" and "book language," poor self-concept, negative attitude toward school, and a curriculum that is foreign to their background and interests. While the language spoken by some learners is a nonstandard variety of English, there is sufficient language learning for initiating reading instruction. For the divergent dialect speaker, language experience instruction can provide materials using the learner's language patterns. Serwer advocates the use of "language engendered by the experience and verbalization of the child as a basis for the reading process." She elaborates further,

> It is safe to say for *beginning* literacy that the child must learn to read in his own dialect or in his first language if it is different. The most economical and rational way to accomplish this goal as well as to capture his interest and to engage him on an appropriate level of concept development is by using his own verbalization, ensconced in his ideation, his idiom, his rhythm, and his style. If the child's language is used and instruction in decoding is based on this language, it is reasonable to assume that early reading would be less prone to failure.[21]

Materials in a Learner's Language

One significant advantage of the language experience approach is the use of materials written in the learner's language. A child who speaks a nonstandard variety of the language may have trouble with conventional materials in standard English. However, when language experience materials are used, there can be a match between the reading materials and the reader's spoken language.

Of crucial importance is the acceptance of the disadvantaged child's existing language as reading materials are developed. The intent is to use the present level of language development as communication through which he learns to read. For example, the following story was dictated by an innercity child:

> Her is Mom.
> Her braids my hair.
> Her cleans around.
> Her shouts me to watch Eddie.
> Nothing else.[22]

For this child to have her story recorded using *she* for *her* in the first two sentences would probably result in her reading the printed word *she* as *her*, thus resulting in confusion of word forms. If the pronoun *she* is not in her oral language background, it should not *at this stage* be used in the reading material. Even though the language may differ from some teachers' standards, there is enough language for the child to begin to read.

One caution should be noted here. The materials used should be written with standard spelling even though the child's vocabulary and syntax will be recorded. For example, if a child says *nes* for *nest*, *nest* should be written, but the child can still pronounce it *nes*.

Acceptance by Teachers

Goodman hypothesizes that the biggest problem dialect speakers face in reading instruction is not the use of a divergent dialect but is the rejection of their speech by teachers. He maintains,

> The only special disadvantage which speakers of low-status dialects suffer in learning to read is one imposed by teachers and schools. Rejection of their dialects and educators' confusion of linguistic difference with linguistic deficiency interferes with the natural process by which learning to read is acquired and undermines the linguistic self-confidence of divergent speakers.[23]

The divergent dialect speaker must be recognized as a language user, and her speech must be accepted and built upon in teaching her literacy. It is possible to use the language children already possess as a bridge between oral communication and written language. Recognition of reading as language processing should focus attention on the tasks confronting a reader who must process language information encoded in a language system that she finds difficult to relate to her oral language system. It should be noted that there is a mismatch factor between spoken and written language for all children since written language is never an exact representation of the oral code, but the difference between the two is greater for linguistically different children.

The need for realistic reading programs that offer maximum opportunity to develop the culturally disadvantaged child's ability to communicate is pressing. The language experience approach is one means of providing meaningful reading content. A moving compilation of writings of ghetto children is found in *The Me Nobody Knows,* edited by Stephen M. Joseph.[24] In *Hooked on Books,* by Daniel Fader,[25] personal writing was one feature of a program developed to reach disadvantaged and delinquent youth through exposure to paperback books. The examples included in these two sources show dramatically the relevancy and impact of personal writing for the disadvantaged.

Stauffer and Cramer report,

> When . . . the disadvantaged person is given an opportunity to read accounts that he has produced, which reflect his thinking about things

23

important to him, and which are a part of his direct experience, his progress is often dramatic.[26]

The language experience approach can be an intensive effort to compensate for and to alleviate the major problems of a lack of readiness for reading, the inappropriate story content of reading textbooks, and the oral language differences that handicap culturally disadvantaged children in reading. Through stimulating experiences and intense personal involvement, the language experience approach can introduce reading to disadvantaged children in a personal, communicative, creative, and purposeful manner.

Adult Illiterates

In recent years attention to the problems of adults who are functionally illiterate has increased. Statistics confirm that a large number of adults in the United States are classified as functionally illiterate. The definition of *functional illiteracy* may vary from inability to read above a certain grade level (often cited are fourth, fifth, or eighth grade levels) or a lack of schooling beyond four or five years to a negative response to the question, "Can you read or write?" Depending on definition, the number of illiterates seems to vary from ten to thirty million—yet, in addition to these figures, there are probably many unidentified illiterates. Regardless of definition, it is certain that many adults are in great need of programs designed to develop reading ability.

As the popularity of the language experience approach has increased, applications of this approach have been made to adult populations. The advantages of language experience reading for an adult illiterate are those stated earlier for elementary students. The language facility that adults have is an asset drawn upon in teaching reading, and the desire adults have for relevant content can be met through language experience learning related to occupational concerns and aspirations as well as to other survival needs. It is possible with language experience learning to have appropriate, meaningful, and functional material.

Students' Material

One man with whom I worked in Washington, D.C., created his first reading materials by retelling the telecasts of the Washington Redskins football team's games. Among the first words he learned were *quarterback*, *tackle*, and *touchdown*. During the assisted reading of the third football story, he glanced up and with that flash of insight that is the teacher's reward, he commented, "If you can say it, you can read it!"

In Atlanta, Georgia, Literacy Action, a nonprofit organization that offers free tutoring of those seeking literacy, makes extensive use of language experience instruction for its clientele. One of the most successful practices is the publication of a newspaper composed of contributions of the students of Literacy Action. The adult learners eagerly await publication of their ideas and are highly motivated to read (or have read to them) the products of fellow students. The newspaper, however, is only one part of the language experience instruction, which consists of personally developed materials related to the individual learner's concerns.

Adaptations of language experience approach based on interests of adult students can be made with use of driver's manuals, banking and credit forms, labels, cooking instructions, TV guides, road signs, application forms, menus, and bus schedules. All of these materials fit into the "survival" category, a high priority in a basic literacy program. These materials could be used for discussion that would lead to the writing of students' ideas. The recorded ideas would then be used to teach reading.

An educator noted for his work with illiterates in Latin America, Paulo Friere, stresses that the foundation for humanistic literacy learning is authentic dialogue among the people. The dialogue then becomes the base from which literacy is learned. The examples he gives of books composed by illiterate peasants (whom he calls "sowers of words") are in his words, "simple, poetic, free" and "profound and elegant."[27]

He contrasts the people's authentic creations with the dull materials often used with illiterates:

> Intellectualist prejudices and above all class prejudices are
> responsible for the naive and unfounded notions that the people
> cannot write their own texts, or that a tape of their conversations
> is valueless since their conversations are impoverished of meaning.
> Comparing what the "sower of words" said in the above references
> with what is generally written by specialist authors of reading
> lessons, we are convinced that only someone with very pronounced
> lack of taste or a lamentable scientific incompetency would
> choose the specialists' texts.[28]

Friere strongly advocates drawing the material for instruction from the concerns of those to be instructed. While the structure of the teaching he advocates is not identical to language experience procedures described in this book, much of the basic philosophy is similar.

A major point to remember in instructing adults is that the instruction should be perceived by the adult learners as functional and pragmatic. Content then will not be predetermined but will be developed by the concerns of the individuals. Specific word analysis strategies and acquisition of a reading vocabulary, along with reading for meaning, will be included in adult reading instruction, but this instruction can be initiated with language experience situations.

25

Goals

The goals of the language experience approach are related to the goals of both reading and language arts instruction. The main goal of language experience teaching is to develop students' abilities to communicate through reading and through language. As an approach to reading instruction, the language experience must, like any approach to reading instruction, build children's reading vocabularies, establish effective strategies for independent word analysis, develop comprehension ability, and promote a favorable attitude toward and interest in reading.

The importance of the activities in the total language arts programs should be recognized. For children to meet the goals, James Smith stresses the need for relevant daily experiences. He identifies the goals of language arts programs as:

1. Each child needs to experience language (remarkably, in dynamic and relevant ways, all day, every day, so he can communicate comfortably in every way open to him, and without unnecessary pressures.
2. Each child must acquire necessary communication skills so that he may express himself effectively in all media.
   a. to listen effectively and for a variety of purposes
   b. to speak effectively in many kinds of social situations
   c. to spell acceptably as a social courtesy
   d. to write legibly and with ease
   e. to learn correct word usage as a social courtesy
   f. to use capitalization and punctuation as social courtesy
   g. to use grammar correctly as a social courtesy
   h. to use reference material effectively
   i. to use word forms correctly
3. Each child needs to come to appreciate the beauty of language itself, the effective use of words, and creative ways they may help him express his own original thoughts.
4. Each child needs to find such satisfaction in his communication experiences that he will develop a healthy attitude toward communicating in all media and will develop his communication skills even without the assistance of the teacher.[29]

Applegate offers the following goals for the language arts:

To use words responsibly
To think clearly
To listen imaginatively
To speak effectively
To read thoughtfully
To write creatively
To use mechanics powerfully
To regard good English respectively
To acquaint children with the best (literature).[30]

The preceding goal statements reflect the integration of reading and language instruction. The language experience approach requires that experiences form the base for the use and development of communication abilities in both oral and written language. A successful language experience reading program teaches both reading and language arts in situations in which communication is an integral part and a goal and in which communication abilities are continually being expanded.

Summary

The language experience approach has been increasingly accepted in recent years as a valid method for teaching reading and communication. The language experience approach is employed for prereading and beginning reading instruction, for remedial readers, for culturally and lingustically different children, as a supplement to other approaches, and occasionally with adult illiterates. The teacher must accept the students' existing level of language development and their language patterns as they create their personal reading materials. The primary goal of reading and language arts teaching in the language experience framework is to develop the ability to communicate in all facets of language.

Notes

1. Gertrude Hildreth, "Experience Related Reading for School Beginners," *Elementary English* 42 (March 1965):280–97.

2. Sylvia Ashton-Warner, *Teacher* (New York: Simon and Schuster, 1963).

3. Guy L. Bond and Robert Dykstra. "The Cooperative Program in First Grade Reading Instruction," *Reading Research Quarterly* 2 (Summer 1967):5–142.

4. Hildreth, "Experience Related Reading."

5. Roach V. Allen, "More Ways Than One," *Childhood Education* 39 (November 1961):108–111.

6. Bond and Dykstra, "The Cooperative Research Program."

7. Harry T. Hahn, "Three Approaches to Beginning Reading Instruction—ITA, Language Experience and Basic Readers—Extended to Second Grade," *The Reading Teacher* 20 (May 1967):715.

8. MaryAnne Hall, *The Language Experience Approach for Teaching Reading: A Research Perspective* (Newark, Del.: International Reading Association, 1978).

9. Russell G. Stauffer, *Action Research in L.E.A. Instructional Procedures* (Newark, Del.: University of Delaware, 1976).

10. Robert Dykstra, "Summary of the Second-Grade Phase of the Cooperative Research Program in Primary Reading Instruction," *Reading Research Quarterly* 4 (Fall 1968):65.

11. Gertrude Hildreth, "Early Writing as an Aid to Reading," *Elementary English* 40 (January 1963): 15, 18.

12. Dolores Durkin, "A Language Arts Program for Pre-First Children: Two Year Achievement Report," *Reading Research Quarterly* 5 (Summer 1970): 534–565.

13. MaryAnne Hall, Sara A. Moretz, and Jodellano Statom, "Writing Before Grade One—A Study of Early Writers," *Language Arts* 53 (May 1976): 582–585.

14. Marie Clay, *What Did I Write?* (Auckland, New Zealand: Heinemann Educational Books, 1975).

15. Bond and Dykstra, "Cooperative Research Program."

16. Russell G. Stauffer and W. Dorsey Hammond, "The Effectiveness of Language Arts and Basic Reader Approaches to First Grade Reading Instruction," *The Reading Teacher* 20 (May 1967): 740–46.

17. William M. Kendrick and Clayton L. Bennett, "A Comparative Study of Two First Grade Language Arts Programs—Extended into Second Grade." *The Reading Teacher* 20 (May 1967): 747–55.

18. Elaine C. Vilscek, Donald L. Cleland, and Loisanne Bilka, "Coordinating and Integrating Language Arts Instruction," *The Reading Teacher* 21 (October 1967): 10.

19. Marjorie S. Johnson, "Basic Considerations in Corrective Instruction," in *Corrective Reading in the Classroom: Perspectives in Reading No. 7*, ed. Marjorie S. Johnson and Roy A. Kress (Newark, Del.: International Reading Association, 1966), pp. 64–68.

20. Rosina Spitzer, "Taking the Pressure Off," *Journal of Reading* 19 (December 1975): 198–200.

21. Blanche L. Serwer, "Linguistic Support for a Method of Teaching Beginning Reading to Black Children," *Reading Research Quarterly* 4 (Summer 1969): 458.

22. "Poignant Drawings Are Helping Slum Children Learn to Read," *The Washington Post*, 28 August 1966, Sec. F., p. 13. © The Washington Post.

23. Kenneth S. Goodman with Catherine S. Buck, "Dialect Barriers to Reading Comprehension Revisited," *The Reading Teacher* 27 (October 1973): 6–7.

24. Stephen M. Joseph, ed., *The Me Nobody Knows* (New York: Avon Books, 1969).

25. Daniel N. Fader, *Hooked on Books: Program and Proof* (New York: Berkley, 1968).

26. Russell G. Stauffer and Ronald L. Cramer, "Reading Specialists in an Occupational Training Program," *The Reading Teacher* 20 (March 1967): 528.

27. Paulo Friere, *Cultural Action for Freedom* (Cambridge, Mass.: Center for Study of Development and Social Change and *Harvard Educational Review*, 1970), pp. 24–25.

28. Friere, *Cultural Action for Freedom*, pp. 24–25.

29. James A. Smith, *Adventures in Communication* (Boston: Allyn and Bacon, 1972), pp. 91–93.

30. Mauree Applegate, *Easy in English* (Evanston, Ill.: Row, Peterson and Company, 1960), p. 8.

Suggested Readings

ALLEN, R. VAN. *Attitudes and the Art of Teaching Reading.* Washington, D.C.: National Education Association, 1965. This pamphlet includes background information for the teacher as well as classroom profiles of kindergarten, primary, and remedial reading classes.

HALL, MARYANNE. *The Language Experience Approach for Teaching Reading: A Research Perspective.* Newark, Del.: International Reading Association and ERIC/RCS, 1978. This review of research provides a comprehensive listing and discussion of research in the language experience approach as well as identifying research needs.

HILDRETH, GERTRUDE. "Experience Related Reading for School Beginners," *Elementary English* 42 (March 1965): 280–97. Hildreth offers a thorough presentation of the historical background of the language experience approach as well as giving citations of the early research and programs related to this approach.

SERWER, BLANCHE L. "Linguistic Support for a Method of Teaching Beginning Reading to Black Children," *Reading Research Quarterly* 7 (Summer 1969): 449–67. Serwer explores the linguistic rationale for the language experience approach for the initial teaching of reading to the culturally different.

SPITZER, ROSINA. "Taking the Pressure Off," *Journal of Reading* 19 (December 1975): 198–200. Spitzer gives examples of middle school remedial readers' success with the language experience approach.

STAUFFER, RUSSELL G. *Action Research in L.E.A. Instructional Procedures.* Newark, Del.: University of Delaware, 1976. Stauffer presents summaries of eighteen studies with the emphasis on classroom application of instructional procedures for language experience programs.

_____. *The Language Experience Approach to the Teaching of Reading.* New York: Harper and Row, 1980. Language experience approach procedures are described in detail. In addition to much attention to beginning reading, applications to higher levels are discussed.

WILSON, ROBERT M. *Diagnostic and Remedial Reading for Classroom and Clinic.* Columbus, Ohio: Charles E. Merrill, 1977. Diagnosis and remediation are the major emphases of this informative source on working with problem readers. Numerous language experience applications for remediation are featured.

3

EXPERIENCE STORIES

One of the major types of reading material created by children in the language experience approach is the experience story. Both individual and group stories are widely used. A variation of the group story is the group book that is made from separate pages by different children about a selected topic. This chapter explores individual experience stories, group experience stories, and group books, with emphasis upon the procedures for developing and using them in teaching reading and language.

The *process* of developing and using the story is the most important consideration, not the final product or the form of the story itself. Knowing the procedures should free the teacher to concentrate on the *communication* process in the *formulation* of the content, in the *recording* of the story, and in the *reading experiences* connected with the story. Encouraging thinking is essential in the process of creating experience stories if children are to view the writing process as the use of letter symbols to record thoughts. Ideas, not mechanics of writing, should be the major concern.

Many of the comments for using experience stories apply to the beginning stages of reading instruction, but adaptations can be made for higher levels. Making experience stories at any level follows the sequence of having children express thoughts through speaking, recording these thoughts in printed language, and finally reading the story, with emphasis on communication in each step.

As children mature in language performance and competence and as the number of words they are able to write independently increases, the experience story becomes less teacher-directed and more pupil-directed. The focus changes from complete dependence upon the teacher as recorder to limited teacher assistance and finally to independent writing. Even though the level of material and difficulty of content increase, the values of personal authorship remain. At higher levels, the written story is used less for reading and more for furthering creative expression through written language. (See chapter 4 for a discussion of written expression.)

Group Experience Stories

In developing a group experience story, the children participate in or discuss an event or a selected topic. Their ideas are recorded and then used for reading material. The teacher must consider motivation, discussion of the experience, recording, reading, and follow-up activities. (Follow-up activities related to prereading are discussed in chapter 8, while word analysis strategies are discussed in chapter 9.)

Motivation for Experience Stories

The teacher has the responsibility for providing motivating experiences that are appropriate and worthwhile. Unless story content is perceived as interesting and personal to children, experience stories can be subject to all the criticism of dull content often leveled at basal readers. Hopefully, teachers using the language experience approach will be skilled in drawing from children much lively comment which will result in highly motivating material. The suggestions given here are only suggestions since it is impossible to determine the content of language experience material apart from the group and individuals involved.

Often a live animal is an excellent stimulus for language experience stories—particularly in the beginning stages. Oral discussion seems to flow naturally with animals as the stimuli.

With five-, six-, and seven-year-old children, topics that center around themselves seem to be the most successful in triggering free responses. For that reason, using the open-ended sentence story starters which contain "I" are recommended. For example, topics such as "I like to . . ., I wish . . ., At home I . . ., After school I . . ." are ones to which it is easy for children to respond.

Many opportunities for composing charts will occur in every classroom. Lists of classroom duties, charts of standards, letters to other classes, letters relating to field trips, and weather records are examples of excellent opportunities for using experience stories related to functional situations. However, the majority of the group experience stories will be of the narrative type, which children compose creatively. Trips, pets, classroom events, pictures, holidays, and television provide springboards for discussion for chart stories.

Commercial materials can be used to motivate language experience stories. The language experience programs of the Encyclopaedia Britannica Press contain numerous ideas to help a teacher plan language experience activities.[1] The *Peabody Language Development Kits*[2] are also particularly useful in providing both pictures and ideas for experience stories. Films also serve as a source of motivation.

One technique for motivating experience stories is that of reading a children's literature story to children and then having them discuss and recall some of the ideas of that story to create an experience story. A variation of this would be to have children create their own story about the same topic but with their ideas. The children's books now available that consist of pictures but no words work well to stimulate stories composed by children.

Many teachers are successful in using pictures to get children to express ideas. If that succeeds, fine. One caution with the use of pictures is that children may tend to only describe and may not feel any personal connection with that stimulus and thus may feel less involved than when the story is more related to them.

DISCUSSION WITH EXPERIENCE STORIES

The group discussion that precedes the writing of the children's ideas provides an important language activity. The discussion experience gives children the opportunity to express and hear ideas in oral language. In discussion situations listening habits can be established, and the teacher can observe and evaluate the language facility of the children. It must be remembered, too, that extending both the experience and language backgrounds of children is a prime concern in language arts instruction.

During the discussion a number of pupils can contribute ideas, and the story produced represents the thinking of the different group members. Even when the number of pupils involved is large, the teacher can provide opportunities for all pupils to participate in this type of activity since the class will be writing many chart stories.

For some children the oral part of the language experience activities is particularly important since some children are very much in need of opportunities to increase their ability to express and understand ideas through oral language.

The discussion often seems smoother if it is done before there is any attempt to record the comments. After the objectives of the discussion are accomplished, it seems easier to write the story if each child is asked to tell something he remembers or likes about the topic. After each response, each child's idea is then recorded. This procedure can prevent the first discussion from being choppy if the writing was interspersed with the discussion.

Recording of Group Experience Stories

Using the pupils' language, the teacher records the pupils' ideas on the chalkboard or on chart paper. The teacher should not change their language to meet her standards of "good" English. If desired, a title is selected by the children and then used in the written record. Appropriate punctuation and capitalization are used as needed. Manuscript writing is used with large letters for easy visibility with careful spacing between words so that the beginning reader can see the relationship of one written word for each spoken word. No attempt is made to control the vocabulary or to limit sentence length.

For beginners and remedial students, watching the recording is recommended in order to develop the realization that the print represents their thoughts. The recording of the story should be done immediately following the discussion so that students have reading material produced immediately. While a tape recorder may be helpful as a means for encouraging creation of stories and for motivating reading practice, taping does not allow the students to see that the process of writing demonstrates that thoughts can be represented by printed language.

Ken's Pizza
We went in Miss Nancy's car.
We went inside and saw
them make dough.
We got a piece of dough.
Then we got to see how
they made the pizza.
After we saw how they
make pizza, we saw them
put it in the oven.
Then we sat down.
We ate two pieces.
We had cheese without
no macaroni.

If the original recording was done on the chalkboard, which many teachers feel is faster and best for the initial lesson with an experience story, the teacher should later copy the story on primary chart paper with a felt-tip pen or marker.

33

Reading of Experience Stories

Immediately after the recording, the teacher reads the group experience story. For children in the initial stages of reading, the teacher will emphasize the left-to-right progression across a line of print while reading the story to the group. Then, the teacher may ask the group to read the story with her. Then, a few children may volunteer to read the story individually. Probably, the motivation, oral discussion, and first reading of the story will occur in the first day's work with an experience story. Additional reading of the chart will be done on following days with some of the activities suggested below.

For prereaders and beginning readers, the second day's reading of the story is again done first by the teacher as the children watch. Next the group reads the story with the teacher, and then some children read the story individually with as much teacher assistance as needed. The reading should be successful and not frustrating. Unnecessary frustration can occur when beginners are asked to read a story without first hearing it read by the teacher. I'm reminded of the student teacher who came to me saying that I had said children could read what they had written when she had taken a reading methods course with me. I went to watch her teach a "slow" group of first graders only to notice that after the excellent motivation and discussion, individual children were directed to read the story and balked at this request. By simply changing the procedure to have the story read by the teacher first and then again with the children, it was possible to build successful experiences while also providing some needed repetition.

Follow-up Activities with Experience Stories

A completed experience record is displayed in the classroom and is used again for various reading acitivities. In most cases, three or four days will be the maximum spent with any one chart. It is preferable to write and read many charts rather than to overdrill on a few. The group stories may be collected on a chart rack for reference in the following weeks. Occasionally, there may be a rereading of some charts just for fun. If the charts are available in the class, many children may choose to reread the charts as a free time activity.

Duplicated copies

Duplicated copies of the group stories have many uses. Copies of the stories can be compiled into a class book that will be available in the class library or on the reading table. Word, phrase, and sentence cards which correspond with the chart can be made, and children can match the cards to the story. An envelope of the words for each story in the folder in the reading corner can be made and can be used for independent practice in visual discrimination. Children can also work independently with matching words and phrases if they are given two duplicated copies and are asked to cut out individual words to match to words in that intact copy. For children who have not yet begun to read, group charts can be used to provide practice in letter discrimination and association of a letter name with the letter form. Children can match letter cards to letters on charts and can name letters in the experience stories. In the follow-up activities, children can frame certain words with an index card with a window cut in it as a teacher may show words on the group chart or as she just says certain words.

After a class has created a group experience story, some students choose to illustrate it as a follow-up activity.

Each child should keep a folder with a copy of each group experience story and the folder will, in effect, be one of his reading books. On the second day of working with a group experience story, each child should be given a duplicated copy of the story. With this copy a child can underline every word she knows, match word cards to the copy, reread the story, illustrate the story, and participate in other teacher-directed acitivities. Additional reading practice occurs when children work in pairs to read the stories to each other or when by choice they reread the stories in the folder. Drama and art are highly motivating creative activities for children. These can be excellent follow-up activities and the motivators for creating experience stories.

PARENTS

In addition to the copies used at school, copies of experience stories may be taken home by children to read with their parents. A note of caution is in order here. Parents should be told how to help their children with the stories and also should know how much is expected of the children. Many teachers

35

find it advisable to send a letter to parents informing them of the procedures to be followed and of the purpose of the stories in the reading program. For beginners, teachers usually recommend that children listen to the parents read the story first before children read it with the parents and then alone. Parents usually appreciate being informed too that any underlined words are words that the child is expected to know. These parent letters can change throughout the year as the instructional emphases change.

The following letter shows a kindergarten teacher's communication with parents for the purpose of encouraging children's efforts at writing. This teacher sends notes throughout the year to build parental understanding of her program, as well as to promote encouragement of children's efforts.

Dear Parents:

A few words about your child's first attempt at writing his or her own "stories" . . .

So that s/he will become a responsible thinker and speller, I will encourage him or her to spell as best s/he can. My comment will be, "It isn't exactly correct, but it's good enough for now; I can read it and so can you. When you next find the word somewhere, look at it and see how close to correct you were." The research I've read indicates that if they correct themselves, they'll remember better than if we furnish the correct spelling.

In the beginning, their words may contain mostly consonants because they hear them more readily. Gradually, they will add vowels—often mixing them up. Please praise their achievements—it's not easy in the beginning! But do encourage writing: letters to relatives, grocery lists, notes to friends, etc. You'll be delighted by the results! Writing promotes reading and vice versa, and at this age it's all very exciting!

Sincerely,

Sheila Murphy
Briar Glen School
1800 S. Briarcliffe Blvd.
Wheaton, Illinois 60187

The stories can also be used in the development of class or individual word banks as pupils identify words of various categories (See pp. 76–78.) For example, a chart about the leaves in the fall could be used to start a classification of color words. Animal, action, and naming words would come from the experience stories. If a child can read a word or words in a group story, those words can be added to his individual word bank.

Stauffer suggests dividing a first grade class into groups and developing experience stories with each. The pace of the instruction and the extent of follow-up activities will vary depending upon the ability of the group.[3]

An Example of
a Group Experience Story

The following story was dictated by a first grade class during the first week of school.

The Rabbit's Nature
He eats carrots and cabbage.
He's lonesome when his mother is away.
He doesn't go anywhere.
He looks black.

The title was a surprise to the teacher, but when the child who suggested it was asked why he wanted that title, he replied, "Well, the story tells what the rabbit is like!" The story was recorded with the children's language exactly as they said it. The contractions were used since they were a part of the children's speech. No attempt was made to repeat or change vocabulary.

Often in the beginning stages, children's names are used in the writing of the story. For example, the story could have been written in a form such as: Brian said, "He eats carrots and cabbage."

In this instance the motivation was the live animal. It triggered a lively discussion that was followed by the teacher's recording of the children's dictated ideas. Next, the teacher read the story to the group, and then the children read the story with her. Additional reading of the chart occurred in the subsequent three days in conjunction with follow-up activities. Copies were made for each child and were also used for follow-up activities.

Other Applications of
Group Experience Stories

Although group charts may not be as widely used after the first half of grade one, some children are still operating at the prereading and beginning stages of reading well into grade one and beyond. For these students, the group experience stories are particularly valuable. Most children, however, will have progressed to a combined approach using language experience materials along with basal readers and library books. Beyond the beginning stages of reading, the group chart serves as a functional language activity and can be a record of important events within the class.

37

Edwards describes the following five-step procedure for using the approach in a group situation with remedial students who were either disadvantaged adolescents or functionally illiterate adults.

1. The teacher stimulates and guides a discussion of a topic or experience.
2. The group's ideas are recorded (by one or all members).
3. Logical sentences and paragraphs are constructed from the randomly recorded thoughts.
4. There is silent reading of the entire selection after it has been duplicated for all students.
5. A variety of follow-up activities can be conducted by small groups or individual students.[4]

The teaching of vocabulary, pronunciation, comprehension, and word analysis is incorporated as needed in the above sequence especially at steps three and five.

The group experience story approach can be adapted for teaching manuscript writing in grade one. The teacher will need to explain that what they write will be much shorter than a chart story but that they can write their own ideas. There will be oral discussion of an experience or idea to determine the statement the children want to record. For instance, the rabbit story on p. 37 could serve as the stimulus with a short sentence such as, "The rabbit hops" or "The rabbit is black" selected for the writing activity. The teacher will demonstrate on a chalkboard, large writing paper, or a transparency for the overhead projector the formation of each letter as the children copy the letters from their individual papers. After the writing, the sentence is read so children feel that their writing communicates an idea. In the stages of first learning to write, the sentence will probably consist of only three or four words. As skill in writing develops, the length of sentences and the stories will increase. However, many children attempt to write and choose to write long before direct teaching in the mechanics of handwriting. No limits should be placed on the length of the self-directed writing efforts. (See pp. 48–49 on early writing.)

Individual Experience Stories

The concept that his speech can be put into written form is a key one for a child using the language experience approach and is best developed through the personal experience story. Personal stories have the same advantage of the group stories and probably stimulate more interest in reading because of the greater personal involvement.

Often children are familiar with the procedures for developing a group story before they compose individual stories. Therefore, they are familiar with the practice of talking about an experience or idea and seeing the thoughts encoded into written symbols that they can then read. As was true for group stories, in using individual stories, the teacher must consider motivation, discussion, recording and reading of the stories, and follow-up activities.

Motivation and Discussion

Many times the motivation for individual stories is conducted with the total class or a subgroup as the teacher presents an idea, topic, or picture for discussion. Discussions preceding the development of individual stories are necessary to promote the language development of some pupils and to encourage thinking. Through questioning, the teacher seeks pupil interest and response. The teacher may use a picture or object to ask, "What do you see?" "What does this make you think of?" "What happened first?" "What happened next?" "What would you like to do?" Trips, pictures, individual experiences, events, literature, art work, birthdays, pets, and special interests can provide the theme for an individual story.

Recording

As was true with the group experience stories, the student should observe the recording of his story. A child should be encouraged to tell a story idea by idea instead of word by word. Sometimes children tend to dictate word by word thinking it may be easier for the recorder, but this pattern may result in unnatural reading.

These stories are usually recorded in manuscript writing or with a primary typewriter. Teachers may choose the form easier for themselves while recognizing that the young reader may prefer the typewritten form since it is more like the print in books. The recorded story should be in such a form as to create pride in its author. A uniform size is desirable if pupil folders of class books are to be compiled with the various stories. In some schools teacher aides or upper grade children are available to record children's dictated stories.

Reading the Story

Immediately after the recording of an individual story, the teacher reads the story to the child. (After the beginning stages of instruction, reading by the teacher can be omitted.) The teacher and child read the story together, and then the pupil can read it alone with teacher help where needed. Next the teacher asks the child to identify the words he can read in the story. As the child says he knows a particular word, the word is written on a card for his word bank.

39

After children have some words in their reading vocabularies, the teacher does not have to hear all the reading of all stories written by the pupils. As the language experience approach is used with other approaches beyond the beginning stages, the children will read many materials in addition to the personal stories. Then the personal stories become more important as an outlet for creative expression rather than as a means of teaching initial reading. The creative stories can be shared in small group settings so that children have an opportunity for oral reading and for hearing the creative work of their peers.

Independent Activities

After the stories have been recorded and read with the teacher, the child works independently with his story. The activity depends upon the child's stage of development. At first he can underline or circle those words that he can identify or had identified with the teacher during the first reading session. The words he can read will become part of his word bank. He can take the word cards from his bank and use them for visual discrimination practice and for word recognition practice as he matches the words in his bank to words in his story. At later stages of development, the reader can identify the words he does *not* know. The latter procedure is followed only after he can recognize all but a few of the words in the story.

Illustrating stories

Illustrating stories is a popular activity for children and adds to the appeal of the finished product. In fact, pupil illustrations provide one of the strongest reasons for producing personal materials. It is the illustrations, too, as well as the thoughts expressed, that contribute to the individuality of the stories. Often personal experience stories will originate from illustrations. Children's drawings can serve as the stimuli for creating a story. Teachers may find for pupils who are reluctant to create stories that having them tell a story about their pictures is the easiest way to begin pupil authorship.

Many teachers have used Polaroid cameras to quickly produce pictures for personal stories. The personal response to pictures of themselves triggers story writing from some children who may not react to any other motivation.

Personal book

Some kindergarten and first grade teachers have an individual conference with each child the first week of school. The child is encouraged to talk about herself, and the teacher writes the child's comments. At the conclusion of the conference, each child has a personal book. The book may be titled with the name of the child or titles such as "About Me," "My Story," "A Story about_____."

40

Displays

Often the teacher may want to display children's illustrated stories with appropriate captions on bulletin boards. A feeling of pride and achievement results when a child realizes that her story is valued enough to be used for classroom display. The bulletin board displays can make children want to read their stories to their classmates, thereby providing additional reading practice.

After individual stories are written, pupils can keep them in a folder. Some teachers make carbon copies when typing the stories for the children for evaluation of the child's progress or for display.

Sharing

When the children have written and read the individual stories, the teacher may form small groups for the sharing of stories. Oral reading can be stressed in this audience type situation, and personal accomplishment will be felt. The teacher is available to help with difficult words so that no child is placed in a situation where she will be unsuccessful. Listening habits are practiced in a functional situation. Children can tape their stories, and the recordings can be used in the listening center.

Individual stories can be placed in the reading corner for independent reading by the rest of the class. Occasionally, the stories can be shown with an opaque projector for reading. The teacher can invite children from another class to hear a group of children read their stories. Sometimes the stories are collected for a class book. The library shelves in the class can include a section of children's stories. In some schools, children's original stories have been placed in the school's central library collection.

Having blank booklets already prepared may serve as an invitation to write for some children. A few pages of blank newsprint stapled together with construction paper covers should be part of the supplies available in a writing center. Chapters 4 and 6 also contain suggestions for stimulating the writing of individual stories.

Group Books

Another popular type of pupil-developed reading material is the group book that is produced by combining the efforts of a number of pupils. Usually the group books are comprised of collections of pages on the same topic by different children. At higher levels as the group books are related to content in social studies and science, each page may deal with a different aspect of an identified topic. Some group books may be written as follow-ups to children's literature materials. Others may be collections of children's creative stories. Some will develop from class discussions, while still others will be outgrowths of study in other curriculum areas. Group books are an excellent source of pupil-composed material for the classroom reading corner.

41

Since group books are cooperative efforts, the motivation and beginning discussion of the content ordinarily will be in a group setting. In the beginning stages of reading instruction, group books may consist of one sentence with an illustration for each page. For example, one first grade teacher was discussing the color red and had the children draw a picture and dictate a sentence about something that was red. The book had a red construction paper cover and was called "Red Things." Some sentences were, "The sun at night is red," "My dress is red," and "A crayon is red." At a more advanced level the books can contain more involved content about more advanced topics and are often written as committee projects related to content areas. These books can be a means of functional writing and reading when pupils use them for recording and reporting information to their class-mates. For example, if the class had been studying a science unit on electricity, a group book on this topic could be written with each child reporting different information pertinent to the unit.

As children illustrate their respective pages, the teacher can record the accompanying sentences while circulating among the group. For reason of motivation, each child's page or contribution should be labeled with his name. The books can be easily assembled by using loose-leaf metal rings. The teacher will read the finished book to the class and may ask each child to read his page. After the books are completed, they should be displayed on the library table for independent reading by children during their free time. Copies of the books can be duplicated for each child. Word cards from the group books should be made available on the same table. Some group books may be donated to the school library. The group books can be used for word study as children select words to be added to the class word bank(s) and as individual children identify known words to be added to their personal banks.

For children who are having difficulty with reading in the content areas of science and social studies, the language procedures for pupil-composed materials can be particularly useful. For example, with a particular topic, the teacher could provide the interest for learning by a field trip, pictures, a film strip, or by conducting an experiment. The next step would be oral discussion of the experiences and content. Pupils' ideas are recorded, and the content is then in their language and is available as reading material. As additional experiences occur, more material written by pupils will be developed. In effect, pupils create their own texts.

In motivating experience stories with children with limited experience backgrounds, a teacher may direct the discussion more specifically and may narrow the topic considerably. For example, a simple question can be used that relates to something very concrete and personal within the realm of children's experiences. Questions such as the following could be asked:

What is your name?
What things are green (red, yellow, etc.)?
Where do you live?
Who is your friend?

What do you like to do?
Who is in your family?
How old are you?
What do you like to eat?
What color is your shirt?
What did you see on your way to school?

Many additional questions of this nature could be posed, and in many cases, a one sentence answer could constitute the entire individual contribution to a class book in the beginning stages. In using this technique, the teacher must be careful not to limit children's talking to this type of expression but should realize that this technique can be a way of starting to put children's speech into written form.

Personal stories, bulletin board displays, group books, and group charts could be developed in connection with each of the topics suggested previously.

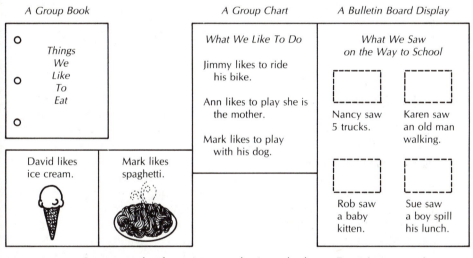

A Group Book *A Group Chart* *A Bulletin Board Display*

Some words of caution may be in order here. Experience stories can be fresh and original, but they can also be trite and stilted. The secret behind imaginative material lies in the teacher's ability to free children to express themselves naturally. With a list of suggested story topics, there is the danger that the list may not relate to the interests of a particular group of children. Controlling or predetermining the content is not congruent with the language experience philosophy.

There is a danger, too, that experience stories can become stale and dull for children. If too much repetition occurs, then the productions may lose their appeal. Perhaps it is better to write too many stories than to drill too much on each story. Some stories will be less interesting than others; for certain stories the follow-up activities can be minimized. Not every follow-up activity is suggested for every story.

Another danger with language experience reading is that there may not be sufficient repetition of mastery of vocabulary and certain reading strategies. The use of follow-up activities for rereading is a way of providing such mastery.

The follow-up activities should be planned carefully so that objectives can be met. For example, if the objective is to have the child to be able to match word, phrase, and letter cards, then the child's demonstration of that behavior should be carefully observed. Certain skill instruction may need to be provided in situations in addition to these activities.

Oral Reading

Helping children communicate through expressive oral reading is another concern of the teacher of elementary reading. Oral reading in the elementary school should occur in functional situations and should not be done in a mechanical or routine manner or only as part of basal instruction.

Advantages

The language experience approach has distinct advantages for teaching oral reading. This approach, which uses children's spoken language, presents an excellent means for helping children realize that in reading they must supply the intonation of spoken language. Instead of working with unnatural word-by-word recitation of controlled vocabulary materials, the teacher can teach oral reading from the beginning stages as a way of making print sound like the spoken language. Sentence patterns that are already in a child's speech form the basis for reading words in meaningful sentence patterns with the characteristic juncture, pitch, and stress normally employed in speech. For children whose language may not match many standard materials, their own experience stories are particularly important since reading textbooks may not reflect their experience background or language use, making the task of reading especially difficult. From the time of the recording of the first group and individual experience stories, the teacher should demonstrate fluent oral reading when reading the stories to the children. Although some teachers tend to read in such a way as to distort the speech patterns with their desire to have children observe individual words carefully, word-by-word emphasis is to be avoided. Children should use expressive reading naturally as they read print that was originally an oral story.

Gradually, discussion of punctuation clues for intonation will occur through the individual and group pupil-composed materials. The function of punctuation is shown as the teacher points out, "This is the end of your thought, so we'll put a period or a dot. The next line is a new sentence, so it will begin with a capital letter." Instruction of this nature should not overshadow the writing and reading experience but can be included occasionally.

Oral reading should be taught since it requires some skills in oral communication in addition to the other reading skills. The teaching of oral reading requires more than merely saying the content of instructional reading materials aloud.

Meaningful oral reading can be provided easily with language experience teaching since children are usually eager to share their creative efforts with others. Audience type situations, such as reading the individual and class books to other classes, can demonstrate the importance of effective oral reading. Small, flexible groups can be formed within classes for sharing stories. As children read their own and their classmates' stories, they can practice effective oral reading. Children can tape their stories, and the tapes can be replayed for personal evaluation of the oral reading.

Silent reading should receive greater emphasis than oral reading since too much emphasis on the latter can be detrimental to the development of a satisfactory rate of silent reading. Since oral reading without meaning is a barrier to comprehension and since the majority of reading tasks require silent reading, such emphasis is essential. In the language experience activities as well as in experiences with other reading materials, children should first read silently that which they are asked to read aloud. Oral reading serves as a diagnostic tool for the teacher as she notes indications of difficulty and analyzes patterns of errors or particular weaknesses.

SUMMARY

Group and individual experience stories and books are the major types of pupil-composed materials in the language experience approach. The procedures for developing these materials are similar since attention is given to motivation, discussion, recording, reading, and follow-up activities for each. The motivation and discussion that precede the recording of pupils' thoughts are stressed, and the recording must be in their language. Reading of the material should occur immediately after its creation, and follow-up activities should be provided for extra practice, direct teaching of selected strategies, and some purposeful oral reading. The focus is on the acceptance of the children's language through functional and creative aspects of the experience stories in the total classroom program.

NOTES

1. Roach V. Allen, *Language Experiences in Reading* (Chicago: Encyclopaedia Britannica Press, 1974).

2. Lloyd M. Dunn and James O. Smith, *Peabody Language Development Kits,* Levels I, II, III (Minneapolis: American Guidance Service, 1965, 1966, 1967).

3. Russell G. Stauffer, *The Language Experience Approach to the Teaching of Reading* (New York: Harper and Row, 1980), pp. 79–89.

4. Thomas J. Edwards, "The Language Experience Approach on Cultural Deprivation," *The Reading Teacher* 18 April 1965):546–51.

Suggested Readings

ALLEN, ROACH V. *Language Experiences in Communication.* Boston: Houghton Mifflin, 1976. Allen's comprehensive book contains numerous examples of child-authored materials along with extensive discussion of the many parts of a language experience program.

_____, and ALLEN, CLARYCE. *Language Experience Activities.* Boston: Houghton Mifflin, 1976. Teachers will find this collection and explanation of ideas very helpful in creating and using experience stories with children.

ARMSTRONG, MARY K. "First Grade Lift-off with Library Books and Lots of Energy," *The Reading Teacher* 27 (May 1974):778–80. A description of first grade language experience activities is the focus of this article. Teachers will find the suggestions for motivating stories and for providing literature experiences helpful.

ASKLAND, LINDA C. "Conducting Individual Language Experience Stories," *The Reading Teacher* 27 (November 1973):167–70. This article contains detailed directions for helping aides to work with individual experience stories.

HERRICK, VIRGIL E., and NERBOVIG, MARCELLA. *Using Experience Charts with Children.* Columbus, Ohio: Charles E. Merrill, 1964. Detailed instructions for constructing and using experience charts with children are described. The illustrations depicting examples make this a valuable resource for the teacher who is learning how to use experience charts. Many types are discussed with application to various curriculum areas and grade levels.

LEE, DORRIS M., and ALLEN, ROACH V. *Learning to Read through Experience.* New York: Appleton-Century-Crofts. 1963, pp. 30–73. Lee and Allen describe both the types and uses of charts as they explain the place of experience stories in reading.

STAUFFER, RUSSELL G. *The Language Experience Approach to the Teaching of Reading.* New York: Harper and Row, 1980. In chapters 2 and 3, Stauffer discusses the use of experience stories in beginning reading. Many examples and detailed procedures are included.

4

Written Expression in the Language Experience Approach

Writing and reading are inextricably interwoven in language experience learning. Children learn literacy through both. Using written language to convey meaning requires the *expression* of meaning through writing as well as the *reception* of meaning through reading. The language experience learner is a writer. The writing itself serves to define, clarify, and transmit meaning. Until recently, most discussion of language experience teaching has centered around reading material created by the author(s) instead of examining the nature of the writing process, the development of competence in written expression, and the contribution of writing to reading.

This chapter explores the connections between writing and language experience learning and teaching. This includes early writing, the writing process including revision, proofreading, editing, spelling, and suggestions for publishing. This chapter on written expression is related to the chapters on vocabulary, literature, and comprehension, since these four program components are often integrated in language experience programs.

Written expression is a component of language experience programs at all levels. Written expression does not begin after children have learned to write or spell; instead, writing is part of the prereading and beginning reading stages. The process itself, the pride in authorship, and acquisition of the craft and tools of an author are central in the writing featured in language experience programs.

Written expression is used here as communication of the author's thoughts—communication that can be purely personal (read only by the author), communication that can be shared with others, and communication that is in conventional forms such as letters and reports. Written expression learning will also include the functional learning of tools of spelling, punctuation, and capitalization.

Early Writing

For some children, learning to write is a harbinger of reading. Children attempting to copy signs or labels or make letter forms usually find writing intriguing as they experiment with pencils, crayons, and paper. Even as children who appear to be scribbling say, "This says . . ." are reflecting, however simple, a grasp of the concept that marks on paper represent ideas.

That many children are interested in and do learn to write in the preschool years has been documented by several researchers.[1,2,3,4] Clay observes, "Somewhere between three and five years most children in a literate culture become aware that people make marks on paper purposefully."[5] Still talking about preschool children, she refers to the "creative urge for children to write down their own ideas."[6]

Early attempts at writing reflect children's attempts to communicate. For example, Hall, Moretz, and Statom report that three-, four-, and five-year-old writers were writing letters to grandparents and to friends who had moved, making birthday cards, playing school with older siblings, and the like.[7] For the children in this study, writing was an attempt to communicate. These writing activities with print have relevance for approaching reading as a communication task.

Read investigates the "spontaneous spelling" used by preschool children in their attempts to write.[8] Of interest is Read's comment that parents of preschool writers ". . . were quite tolerant of their children's spelling efforts."[9] Graves urges that teachers accept children's spontaneous or invented spelling and recognize such spelling as a step toward mastery of the complex English orthographical system.[10]

Writing for some children precedes reading. The orientation to, experience with, and interest in print developed through writing can help in learning to read. A child's attention to features of letters in the attempts at copying relates to the discrimination of distinctive features of letters and words in reading. Another advantage of writing for young children is the active involvement of the learner. Writing for some early learners is a self-directed activity.

Language experience charts and stories for young children who have not yet begun to read provide exposure to and introduction to print as a

48

natural part of the learning environment. Many children will choose to try to write for themselves when they see print used in relevant ways, when their names are printed in the classroom, when their dictation is recorded for their art work, when many signs and captions are evident, and when classroom events and procedures are charted as appropriate. Children who are exposed to print in relevant, functional ways will be curious about that print and will often select writing as an appealing, independent activity.

The Writing Process

The process of writing deserves as much attention as does the final product. Although the evidence of children's communicative efforts can be found most easily in their actual products, the process that leads to the product is of concern to teachers. Donald Graves has researched the actual writing process of elementary students and is continuing to research elementary students' behavior while engaged in writing. Among his findings in a study reported in *Research in the Teaching of English* are the following:

1. Informal environments give greater choice to children. When children are given choice as to whether they write or not as to what to write, they write more and in greater length than when specific writing assignments are given.
2. Results of writing done in the informal environments demonstrate that children do not need motivation or supervision in order to write.
3. The formal environments seem to be more favorable to girls in that they write more, and to greater length, than do boys whether the writing is assigned or unassigned.
4. The informal environments seem to favor boys in that they write more than girls in assigned or unassigned work.
5. In either environment, formal or informal, unassigned writing is longer than assigned writing.
6. An environment that requires large amounts of assigned writing inhibits the range, content, and amount of writing done by children.
7. The writing developmental level of the child is the best predictor of writing process behaviors and therefore transcends the importance of environment, materials, and methodologies in influence on children's writing.[11]

Important in Graves's findings is the lack of need for contrived motivation or the assignment of specified topics. He is reporting that children who feel they have something to say, who feel that it is valued and accepted, and who are given time and an encouraging setting will write and will write extensively. Through the extensive writing comes discovery of how written language functions. It is important to remember that children learned oral

49

language as it was functional in their environment. Children need the opportunities for discovery and extensive use with written language, too.

Underlying Principles for Teaching Written Expression

Certain conditions foster creativity in children; others stifle it. Torrance finds that teacher personality and classroom environment affect the children's creative performance.[12] In developing an effective instructional program of creative writing, the following principles should be remembered.

Acceptance

An atmosphere of acceptance and freedom is essential. Teachers must believe that each child has the potential to be inventive and productive. At all levels, an atmosphere that encourages, nurtures, and welcomes original expression must be present if children are to grow in their ability to use written language expressively and effectively. What children write must be accepted and valued by the teacher. Children must feel secure to try new ideas and unusual thoughts and to experiment with writing. All children in the elementary school cannot be expected to be gifted writers, and even children who write well will not produce quality writing every time, but all children should feel that their contributions are accepted. Climate and the process of self-expression are more important than a polished product.

Individual evaluation

Evaluation of pupils' writing should be on an individual basis. Creative writing should not be graded. Burrows writes, "The quality and sincerity of child writing dwindles to nothing if fear and self-consciousness set in."[13] If children feel that set standards must be met each time they write and if their writing is to be graded, their freedom to create is blocked. Myers and Torrance talk of "time to think without being threatened by grades or tyrannized by time."[14] Evaluation occurs as children keep individual folders of stories and note improvements. Teachers may keep individual records of pupils' writing and note the qualities of originality, richness of expression, word quality, organization, and imagination. Occasionally, classes should talk about qualities or characteristics of good writing so that children will have some criteria for individual evaluation.

Freedom of choice

Children should be free to select their topics and to determine length and form. Since writing is personal, as the child puts down what he feels and thinks, he selects the words used and the ideas communicated. When children write, topics should be open-ended with freedom of choice. Children also should have the option of choosing *not* to write.

Motivation, discussion, and sharing

Instruction in written expression consists of more than having children record their thoughts. Time must be spent on motivation, discussion, and sharing as well as on writing. Since children must have ideas and experiences from which to create, the teacher has a responsibility for providing experiences and models that children can draw upon for their own creative efforts. To develop pride of authorship, pupils need to share their writing with others and to have some of their stories and poems included in a class or individual book, a class newspaper, or in a bulletin board display.

Conducting Writing Experiences

In classrooms where children are encouraged to write extensively and early, writing is usually a component or extension of many other activities and is a result of students having something to communicate related to the substantive content and experiences of that class. While contrived experiences are not the best way to promote facility in written expression, it is possible for teachers to plan worthwhile experiences to motivate writing.

The writing process and the teaching of that process consists of more than the actual minutes spent putting pen or pencil to paper. Prior to the production of written language is the precomposing step of idea generation, and the initial composing is followed by examination leading to revision, editing, and proofreading.

Teachers will find numerous suggestions for motivating writing in the supplementary readings cited at the end of this chapter. It should be stressed that one of the teacher's primary obligations in promoting creativity is to provide a supportive environment and to generate ideas and enthusiasm. Some of the proven means for encouraging thought on a particular topic are

1. Presenting a children's literature story or poem
2. Showing some appealing pictures
3. Asking stimulating questions
4. Suggesting and exploring imaginative topics

However, regardless of the effectiveness of the motivation or technique used, children often are asked to write before thinking is truly stimulated. Thus, creative writing becomes an assignment instead of a language and thinking experience.

Discussions should be held before children are directed to write their ideas. Questions of "How does this look?" "How does it make you feel?" "What can you see, hear, or touch?" "What are some interesting words you would want to use to describe what you see, hear, and feel?" stimulate thought. Children can react in an oral situation and can see that their responses are accepted. In the discussion the teacher should make many accepting comments such as, "That's a fine idea; you can use it in your

51

story," or "That's an interesting way to describe what you feel. Can you include that when you write your ideas?" or "That's a sentence with lots of action; your story will probably be an exciting one." With comments of this nature, the children will feel encouraged to express their ideas. Another result of the discussion stage should be the understanding that many types of stories and varied topics are acceptable. Even though the motivation and discussion may have concentrated on a single subject, students are encouraged to develop that topic from various angles. It is suggested that the teacher tell the children they can write about any of the ideas discussed or about something else if they wish. This type of comment emphasizes the open-ended dimension of the topic. Pupil choice must be respected. Generally, if an idea is well presented and appealing to children, they will be content to write about it. However, children should be free to approach any topic in a variety of ways or to write about something else if they choose to do so.

As children write their stories, the teacher can be available for help with words as needed. When a child asks how to spell a word, it is advisable for the teacher to write the word for her to copy. Every teacher is probably familiar with the situation in which a word is spelled orally, and the child asks the teacher to repeat the spelling with the requested words sometimes still incorrect in the child's story. The cards for the requested words can be put in the child's word bank, and the individual banks can be used as references during creative writing. With all the stress frequently put on the mechanics of writing and on the correctness of written work, it is recommended that the motivation for writing not be lessened by reminding children to spell and write correctly immediately before starting their stories.

A children's literature story encourages creative writing by this child.

The sharing of writing provides a setting for functional listening, speaking, and oral reading. Small groups can be formed for pupils to read their stories to each other, or the teacher can read (with the writer's consent) the stories to the group. Often when the teacher reads very expressively, children are surprised at how much their stories say. During the sharing periods, the teacher can comment on the good qualities of the stories mentioned in the discussion. Again, the focus is on acceptance and on language awareness stemming from the pupils' existing use of language. Sharing through displays should also be included. Collections of children's stories should be available in the classroom library and reading center, and stories can be taped and available in the listening center.

A Sample Creative Writing Experience

Background

The experience described here occurred in a fifth grade class, and the examples of the children's writing are exactly as they recorded them. *The Sun Is a Golden Earring,* by Natalia Belting,[15] was the only material needed other than pencils and paper for writing. In addition to developing creativity through writing and enjoying literature, the objectives of this lesson were for children to be able

1. To identify expressive words and phrases in order to develop language awareness,
2. To write a story or poem using descriptive words,
3. To express their thoughts in written language.

Motivation

The teacher introduced the book by explaining that *The Sun Is a Golden Earring* is a collection of short myths and legends from around the world about heavenly bodies and weather. These legends were told by ancient peoples to explain phenomena they could not understand.

The title was discussed as a comparison, and the pupils were asked to listen for other comparisons in the book. The teacher wrote these questions, "What words help you see how something looks?" "What words tell how something sounds?" She then read the book aloud without any discussion during the reading.

Discussion

The teacher asked what comparisons the students noticed, and they mentioned, "The sky is a tent roof," "The stars are a woman's necklace," and "The rainbow is a fishing line of the king of the dragons." The questions listed under motivation were discussed.

After talking about the book, the children were asked if they could describe the things in the sky or the kinds of weather. Gradually, pupils began to volunteer ideas. With each suggestion, praise and acceptance were given. Many times the teacher would say, "That's an interesting description," or "That's a good word to use to describe the way that looks." The discussion was a warming-up period to help children formulate their ideas and realize that their suggestions would be accepted.

Writing

Before the children started to write, the teacher reminded them that they had expressed many good ideas which they could use in their stories or descrip-

53

tions. The topic was open-ended, for it was suggested that they could write a brief explanation of how something in the sky came to be or something about weather or something entirely different if they wished.

As the children wrote, the teacher assisted with words that she wrote on small slips of paper for the children's word banks. In no case did she say, "Remember capital letters and punctuation." As she walked around, she made comments such as, "That's a good idea," "You describe that well," "You're off to a good start. Could you tell a little more how that happened or how it looks?" "That's a different idea," and "Good."

Sharing

Children should decide whether or not their work is to be shared with others. In this lesson, the teacher collected the papers and said, "As I was watching you write, I saw many good stories, and I think you would enjoy hearing them. When I come to your paper, will you tell me if I can read your story?" She then proceeded to call each child's name, to read the stories, and to comment favorably on some feature of each child's work. If a child said not to read his, that wish was respected but again a favorable comment was made. Interesting uses of words were noted by the teacher and the children during this sharing session.

After the lesson described here, the children copied and illustrated their stories, which were used for a bulletin board display. Some interesting words and phrases were added to the class compilation. (See p. 60) The book was available for individual reading. In order to provide additional experience with this type of writing, the writing center featured the question, "Can you write a legend about heavenly bodies or about the weather?"

Examples From a Fifth Grade Class

How an Ordinary God Made Lightning

Once a long time ago a very ordinary God wanted to talk to his friends in the sky. So he decided to go and try to talk to the Rain God. Now this very little meak God had never spoken a word before and wondered what it would be like. He thought for a while before he opened his mouth. He thought it might be like a trumpet or like the birds singing in the trees. But when he opened his mouth he found something very different. He could speak just like any other God but he had something special. He found he could flash his teeth as he pleased for they were as bright as the Sun God. When He went to show the other Gods they said he must be the lightning God. And to this day when ever the lightning God talks there is lightning.

Lightning

There was an old lady who lives in the heavens. And all year long she would sit and sew. Sometimes she would drop her needle and it would fall and tear the sky. But then the sky was magic and after it was torn it would heal very quickly and that made Lightning.

Rain

Up in the heavens live an old man. All year long he would sit and smoke his pipe. When he was finished smoking he would shake the ashes out of his pipe. The ashes would fall to the earth. And this made Rain.

Snow and How It Became

Once there was a woman in the heavens who's husband was a god. One day her husband got up early and forgot to make his bed, so his wife had to make it. So she had to change the sheets and pillowcases. (because he slept on 15 pillows.) She went to shake the 15th pillow, which was the largest, and the seam came apart and the little tiny feathers flew down from the heavens. Now the god's wife had to go down and pick it up. And that is how the snow comes and goes.

The Story of Rain

One day a young and beautiful god was walking a long and saw a little boy pick and trample a beautiful flower. When she saw this she began to weep. Now every time a flower is picked anywhere she begins to weep. Her weeping is the rain.

Thunder and Lightning

Thunder is when the footplayers of both teams have the same score. And when one of the kickers of the team kicked the ball it sounded like thunder and it streeked through the sky like lightning and makes the winning point.

Snow

Snow is like a clean white sheet that has fallen across the United States and all the kids are happy. They take their sleds and other things. Then the cne of the old and meanest of all the sun gods took the sheet and wouldn't give it back till next winter.

Thunder, Rain, and, Lightning

One day some angles and some of the gods went bowling. The first angle missed and he started to cry. The next person was a god and he rooled the ball and sparks came and the Bang! all pins fell down the god was so happy the sun came out and the skies were clear again and all the people on earth were happy it stoped thundering, raining and lightning.

How Saturn Got its Rings

Once there was a great Queen who was very mean and she was very gready! She had a very huge chest of rings. In fact she had 100 for every finger. Thoe she was gready she was also as beautiful as the sunrise in the morning coming up over the montains. And she fell in love with a Prince, but he was not gready so he made her give up all her ring but 10 she didn't no what to do with them so she gave them to a planit called Saturn.

Rain

There was a god's wife who was peeling onions and the "fumes" made her cry. We call this rain.

Earth

There was a big turtle that walked in the heavens and one day died and fell into the space which took up the room of the earth and great vines grow and trees grow. Animales and a god lived there. We call it earth.

Hail

Someone from the heavens throwing rocks down to the earth.

The Moon and the Milky Way

Someone poured milk into the moon and it came out the bottom and fell into which we now call the Milky Way. The color white that you still see is the Milk stain which will stay there forever and ever.

How The Clouds Came to Be

The stars are a diamond teakettle and when the gods decide to have tea they boil the tea and steam comes out and forms the clouds.

How Rain, Thunder and Lighting is Caused

There was once a king who was mean and selfish. His palace was on the highest peak in the world. Whe he is mad he walks around and stampes his feet which caues thunder. He is so selfish he drank the all the water in the kingdon spilling haft the water which caues rain. The king's taxes were hight. Lighting was caused by the gold coins, droping from his hand when he is counting it.

Thunder is like a stampid of elephants thundering across the heavens the lightning is there tails flashing across the sky.

Thundering

Thundering is two clouds smashing together. An horses feet claping in heaven And two people fighting and sceaming in heaven.

The Sound of a Horse

When a horse goes trotting in the lomesome dark streets, the hoofs sound like a man running from tearer. And when lighting strikes, the horse get's faster and faster intil it sounds like a tribe of Indians having a war party.

How Rain Developed (a story of the gods)

One day when the earth was being formed it was very hot on earth. One day up in the heaven's a God was watering his lawn with a sprinkler The drops that hit the floor went through and some hissed. So they fell on the earth. Some were stuck in the web that separates earth from the heaven. They made the morning dew. Every time the Cheif God wanted rain he would call the man and tell him to turn on the sprinkler to water his lawn. Thats how rain developed.

P.S. But of course he gets mean and doesn't turn it on. So we have a drought.

Thunder and Lightning

thunder—when a baseball Maneger and the Umpire are argueing and when a baseball player catches a line drive

lightning—when a baseball player hits a homerun and the ball streaks into the stands

When it rain's

1) When it rain's it's like a water sprinkler coming from the sky.

2) It's like dimes falling out of your pocket's, Like pennies gold and silver.

57

Thunder

I think thunder is when two mad scientists get angry when there out in the rain and shoot fifty calibre machine guns hit the clouds and the clouds yell.

Fog is from meteors coming close to earth. The used fuel from the fire on them comes into our atmosphere.

How snow looks to me

It is a God poping pop corn. He has a burning fire and pop corn is falling out. People on earth are grabbing it and eating all they want.

Stars

Stars are white cookies that float in the sky. And Stars are big snow flakes.

Clouds

Clouds are smoke that travle under the sky, which is light.

Clouds And How They Were Formed

Clouds are like smoke from a chimney of a house in the heavens or a horse kiking up dust in the heavens.

What horses look like

Horses look like whitecaps on the dark blue sea. When the whitecaps swirl around madly, horses are galloping. When they're calm horses are trotting. Horses are so swift you can barely see their flying manes and tails which look like breezes blowing the green grass.

The Grass

The grass is like a slimy thin green snakes that have grown from the ground.

The procedure described in the preceding example was used again with the book *The Long-Tailed Bear and Other Indian Legends,* also by Natalia Belting.* The stories in this book are North American Indian tales or "why" stories about animals. The following examples were written after fifth grade children heard "How the Cardinal Got His Red Feathers" taken from this collection.

*Natalia Belting, *The Long-Tailed Bear and Other Indian Legends* (Indianapolis: The Bobbs-Merrill Co., 1961).

How the Cat Got His Fur

One day there was only one cat in the world. It belong to a Barber. The cat always stood right under his masters feet. One day the Barber got a customer who had a lot of hair to be cut. First the Barber had to put a very sticky liquid on the man's head. By accident it fell on the cat so the Barber got another jar. He forgot to wipe the mess up and started cutting the man's hair. The cat rolled into the hair and it stuck tightly. That is how the cat got his fur.

How The Horse Got It's Tail And Mane or
How The Horse Got Short Hair

The horse used to have a very long coat. He was shaggier than a English Sheep Dog. It was summer and as hot as a forest fire. The horse was very hot, so he went to the lion and asked him to cut his coat with his teeth. The lion agreed. It was very cool without his long coat. None of his hair grew back except where his mane and tail are. ——The lion was magic and he knew that the horse would be cold in winter, so the horse's hair grows back in winter and he sheds in the summer.

A White Rabbit and How it got its fur

A white rabbit it is so white it it looks like some snow has fallen on him. And he ran back to the forest and try to shake it off. but it couldn't come off. And it turn in to fur.

How the Fox got the white tip on his tail

A red fox which was as bright as the sunset was walking through the woods He decided to see "Man's House." So he went their. "Man" had just finished painted his house snow white. He left the paint on the steps. Fox accidentally dipped the tip of his tail in the paint That's how the fox got his white tip.

P.S. ALL HER babies were born naturally with white tips.

How the fox got his white tail

The fox was walking though the woods one day. He was very unhappy with his red tail because his red tail was like the red carnidel and the cat would come and jump on them. So he was walking though the wood one day when he saw a can lableed white paint. So he dipped his tail in the paint and he thought that his whole body was white like the saimise cat. He was disapointed when he found out his body wasn't white. He told about it and they thought it looked nice so they dipped theirs in the white paint.

59

> ### *Why Spiders Have Six Legs and Why Some are black*
>
> Once there was a spider that had three children so, she had thre legs. She got the other three legs to mined her white washed web and to wash the dishes and answer the telephone. The nexed day her neighbor sent her child over to play. He was going to put black ink all over them He put black ink on the mother and one child but, he ran out of ink so, the others were brown because that was what coler they relly were.
>
> The End
>
> ### *How Our Hair Got its Color*
>
> Once apon a time there was a little girl with golden braids, named Audrey.
> She was very curious and one day she asked her father why her hair was yellow.
> Her father said, "Well, once there was a little girl with tan hair. She didn't like it she said it looked as though someone didn't wash it good enough.
> One day her mother said, "Go outside and polish the silver lamp.
> While she was polishing it a funny thing happened, smoke rose from it like someone was smoking a pipe inside it. A "jini" appeared and said "You have one wish.
> She quickly said "I wish the fur on heads could be as yellow as the buttercups, as brown as the mud that lies on the earth, as black as the blackbirds or as red as the cardinal's wings are.
> And to this very day those are still the colors of hair!

OTHER TEACHING SUGGESTIONS

Children can start a collection of the interesting language used in their stories. Using their words *verbatim* is an excellent practice since the children will then realize that they can say things in an expressive manner and that their expressions are valued by the teacher and their classmates.

For example, in a second grade class, the children discussed what they would do if they had a hundred dollars to spend. In the individual stories written following the discussion, one boy wrote, "If I had a hundred dollars to spend I'd buy a bike so I could ride up and down the hills like the waves coming in fast." This simile was personal for this child who had had experiences at the nearby Chesapeake Bay. The group discussed why the comparison of the bike ride to the waves made the story more interesting than merely stating, "I'd ride up and down the hills." The sentence was placed on

60

a chart labeled "Interesting Language," and other examples were added each time the group wrote stories. Another example was a description of giving a dog a bath. "His chin had a beard of soap suds." The children in this particular group were highly motivated to express their ideas in interesting ways and enjoyed having their expressions recognized by the total group.

Reading literature to children every day is a source of input that adds to the background for creativity. Writing can follow the reading of certain literature selections. Children need exposure to the ideas of many authors. Discussion of the style, literary devices, and forms of writing can be initiated with literature examples. (See chapter 6.) Stewig's book *Read to Write* describes the use of literature to teach features of writing.[16]

Alerting children to the creative writing of other children available in commercial publications is also recommended. The books *Miracles*,[17] *Journeys*,[18] and *The Wind and the Rain*,[19] edited by Richard Lewis, are excellent examples of children's writing in published form. Hall and Gambrell describe a number of publications in which children are the authors.[20] Children frequently react very favorably to these writings of other children.

Collecting the children's writing and duplicating copies of a class book for each child are other means for maintaining interest in writing. Story starters, such as the open-ended sentences suggested in chapter 3, can be helpful material for a writing center or as the focus for a directed lesson. In classrooms where children are comfortable in expressing feelings, a starter such as "I wish" or "I feel" can result in some probing creative expression.

Inviting other classes to hear children read their original stories and poems usually appeals to children.

Arranging attractive displays of the children's stories on bulletin boards, in classroom reading centers, the halls, and the school library demonstrates that children's efforts are valued and promotes interest in writing.

Some schools and school systems have conducted "Young Authors' Fairs" in which children's works are displayed along with programs that may feature noted authors of trade books or other topics related to encouragement of children's creative efforts. Humphrey and Redden describe a young authors' project that had its purpose to stimulate children to write creatively, to give recognition to children who write, and to provide books for other children to read.[21] They report that the books written by children are very popular with children.

A local author can visit the class to talk about the stages in developing a manuscript. Children can be alerted to the need for proofreading a final copy and to the realization that polished copies come only after considerable rewriting.

For imaginative open-ended ways of stimulating productive thinking and imaginative writing, teachers will want to explore the teacher's guides and pupil idea books by Myers and Torrance.[22] Open-endedness, pupil involvement, and personal reaction and interpretation are distinctive features of all these creative materials. The directions and suggestions are helpful but not prescriptive.

61

ReshapiNq WriTiNq

The term *reshaping* is used by Stewig instead of editing to refer to the conscious process of analyzing and discerning the quality and qualities of writing to help produce even better writing.[23] Reshaping focuses on content and expression of ideas instead of mechanics such as punctuation and capitalization. However, proofreading for correction of mechanics is also taught but is considered as proofreading and not as reshaping.

Teacher-student conferences can help in the reshaping of writing, and students can confer with each other. Questions such as, "What do you like best about this story?" "What does this piece of writing tell you about the author's feelings?" "What description is the clearest?" "Why?" "Is there any part you'd like to change?" aid in personal analysis of a piece of writing. These questions are not meant to be ones where the teacher evaluates but instead ones that assist students in self-examination of their writing.

One idea that helps develop the understanding that revision is part of the writing process is called "the three-lead idea" by Calkins.[24] She describes having third grade students write three beginnings and then select the best of these. In another article, Calkins gives examples of changes in writing that occur through reshaping as children clearly view the revisions as necessary for clear communication.[25] This process is not one of children simply copying a version incorporating the teacher's changes, but one where the writer changes to achieve the desired results.

An important condition for having children learn to reshape is for them to realize that a good paper is not necessarily a neat paper, and that in writing, revision does result in marking, inserting, crossing out, and erasing in order to get the right words and thoughts. The neat product comes when children are displaying and publishing their work for others to read.

PublishiNq

Publishing children's writing promotes great pride in authorship and is a powerful motivator. Publishing conveys that children's writing is important and valued. Publishing also presents a reason for preparing a final reshaped and proofread copy.

Publishing and displaying can take many forms from simply showing children's writing papers on a bulletin board to printing and binding books, which can become permanent parts of school and classroom libraries or treasured personal possessions.

Collections of children's writing can be published frequently in dittoed form as a class magazine. A column in a class or school newspaper can be devoted to publishing children's original stories and poems. School and class newspapers provide a means for modeling varied styles of writing in addition to providing a natural situation for publication.

A publishing or bookbinding center as suggested in chapter 10 is an important feature of language experience classrooms. All students should have some writing selected each year for inclusion in a bound book. Classrooms with teacher aides and publishing centers will probably have a large number of bound books since the teacher will not feel responsible for doing all of the bookbinding.

Some Words of Caution

Teachers are sometimes alarmed about the lack of quality in children's writing, the similarity of content in a particular child's stories, or the tendency of children to imitate other children or a particular book or poem. While a teacher is concerned about these behaviors, the need is to convey an atmosphere of acceptance, to provide stimulation to create in a variety of situations, and to continue to offer exposure to a variety of models. Even though children's stories may not appear unique to adults, the teacher must look for that which is original and new for the child who is writing.

Children should have the opportunity to start over if they decide they do not like a particular story. They must also have the option of rough drafts and be told that frequently a story must be rewritten to make the language and ideas satisfactory. Children should not be forced to write on a particular day if no suggestions appeal to them. Attitude and interest are crucial, and demanding a composition may have many negative results.

While many language experiences will not lead directly to written expression, discussions of words, exposure to the language of literature, and encouraging reflective and divergent thinking are the foundation for imaginative writing. Teachers should be aware that children (like adults) write best about what they know; therefore, writing about personal interests and experiences should not be overshadowed or neglected by the teacher's suggestions.

Spelling

Learning to spell starts with the first attempts at writing. Documentation that spelling begins in the preschool years is found in the work of Charles Read.[26,27] The works of Beers and Henderson [28] and Templeton[29] also show that the so-called spontaneous or invented spelling of children is not random but instead reflects a gradual discovery and development of the patterning of the English orthographical system.

Research on language experience programs shows that children in these programs achieve significantly better on measures of spelling than children in other types of reading programs.[30,31] The extensive experiences with writing are thought to be the major factor in language experience instructed children's good performance in spelling. Children who are actively involved in the *use* and *application* of spelling will see the need for it and will profit from the practice in language experience activities.

Word Banks

Spelling is included in language experience programs through individual word banks for collection of spelling words as needed. (See chapter 5 for a discussion of word banks.) As children request words during writing experiences, the words can be given to them and then become part of the individual spelling word box. When children prepare a final proofread copy of written work for display or publication, the teacher can give them the corrected form of misspelled words on their draft copy, and these words can also become part of the individual spelling collection.

Evaluation

Children's personal independent writing can serve as an excellent source of diagnostic information about children's spelling. The independent writing offers a much more realistic picture of spelling performance than does testing, since the writing reflects application. Teacher evaluation of the spelling errors should consider whether a child is missing words that he should have mastered previously or whether the errors reflect reasonable tries at words not previously used. The evaluation should also consider the developmental predictability of certain errors.

A fetish about correct spelling should not interfere with writing efforts. Children must be encouraged to try to spell words not previously used in writing. When revision is advisable, these attempts and appropriate feedback will aid in acquiring a spelling vocabulary, learning the necessity of spelling, and learning patterns of English spelling.

Summary

Writing experience contributes to the language experience approach to teaching communication. Writing is a corollary of reading in literacy learning. In language experience programs from the prereading level to higher ones, writing and reading are closely related. Through written expression, a teacher seeks to help students express thoughts in fresh and original ways and to increase their power to use language. A directed writing experience includes motivation, discussion, writing, and sharing. Spelling, revising, editing, and publishing are part of the writing component of language experience programs.

NOTES

1. Dolores Durkin, *Children Who Read Early* (New York: Teachers College Press, 1966).

2. MaryAnne Hall, Sara A. Moretz, and Jodellano Statom, "Writing Before Grade One: A Study of Early Writers," *Language Arts* 53 (May 1976): 582–584.

3. Charles Read, "Preschool Children's Knowledge of English Phonology," *Harvard Educational Review* 41 (February 1971): 1–34.

4. Marie M. Clay, *What Did I Write?* (Auckland, New Zealand: Heinemann Educational Books, 1975).

5. Marie M. Clay, "Exploring with a Pencil," *Theory into Practice* 16 (December 1977): 334.

6. Clay, "Exploring with a Pencil," p. 335.

7. Hall, Moretz, and Statom, "Writing Before Grade One."

8. Read, "Preschool Children's Knowledge of English Phonology," p. 8.

9. Charles Read, *Children's Categorization of Speech Sounds in English* (Urbana, Ill.: National Council of Teachers of English, 1975).

10. Donald H. Graves, "Research Update: What Children Show Us About Revision," *Language Arts* 56 (March 1979): 314, 318.

11. Donald H. Graves, "An Examination of the Writing Processes of Seven-Year-Old Children," *Research in the Teaching of English* (Winter 1975): 235. Copyright © 1975 by the National Council of Teachers of English. Reprinted by permission of the publisher and the author.

12. E. Paul Torrance, *Guiding Creative Talent* (Englewood Cliffs, N.J.: Prentice-Hall, Inc., 1962).

13. Alvina Burrows, Doris C. Jackson, and Dorothy O. Saunders, *They All Want to Write* (New York: Holt, Rinehart & Winston, 1964), p. 43.

14. R. E. Myers and E. Paul Torrance, *Teachers Guide, Invitations to Speaking and Writing Creatively* (Boston: Ginn and Company, 1965), p.v.

15. Natalia Belting, *The Sun Is a Golden Earring* (New York: Holt, Rinehart & Winston, 1962).

16. John W. Stewig, *Read to Write* (New York: Hawthorn Books, 1975).

17. Richard Lewis, comp., *Miracles* (New York: Simon & Schuster, 1966).

18. Richard Lewis, comp., *Journeys* (New York: Simon & Schuster, 1969).

19. Richard Lewis, comp., *The Wind and the Rain* (New York: Simon & Schuster, 1968).

20. MaryAnne Hall and Linda B. Gambrell, "Children as Authors," *Elementary English* 49 (October 1972): 889–93.

21. Jack W. Humphrey and Sandra R. Redden, "Encouraging Young Authors," *The Reading Teacher* 25 (April 1972): 643–51.

22. R. E. Myers and E. Paul Torrance, *Invitations to Speaking and Writing Creatively* (Boston: Ginn and Company, 1965): *For Those Who Wonder* (Boston: Ginn and Company, 1966); *Plots, Puzzles and Ploys* (Boston: Ginn and Company, 1966).

23. Stewig, *Read to Write*, p. 221.

24. Lucy McCormick Calkins, in Donald Graves, "Research Update: Andrea Learns to Make Writing Hard," *Language Arts* 56 (May 1979): 569–576.

25. Lucy McCormick Calkins, "Children Write—And Their Writing Becomes Their Textbook," *Language Arts* 55 (October 1978): 804–810.

26. Read, "Preschool Children's Knowledge of English Phonology."

27. Read, *Children's Categorization of Speech Sounds in English.*

28. James W. Beers and Edmund H. Henderson, "A Study of Developing Orthographic Concepts among First Graders," *Research in the Teaching of English* 11 (Fall 1977): 133–148.

29. Shane Templeton, "Spelling First, Sound Later: The Relationship Between Orthography and Higher Order Phonological Knowledge in Older Students," *Research in the Teaching of English* 13 (October 1979): 255–264.

30. MaryAnne Hall, *The Language Experience Approach for Teaching Reading: A Research Perspective* (Newark, Del.: International Reading Association, 1978): 29–30.

31. Ronald L. Cramer, "An Investigation of the Spelling Achievement of Two Groups of First-Grade Classes on Phonologically Regular and Irregular Words and in Written Composition." (Ph.D. diss., University of Delaware, 1968.)

Suggested Readings

BRAUN, CARL, and FROESE, VICTOR, eds. *An Experience-Based Approach to Language and Reading.* Baltimore: University Park Press, 1977. Froese's chapter, "Diagnostic Teaching of Composition," treats the issue of balance on creative expression and mechanics with a discussion of developing composition ability.

CLAY, MARIE. *What Did I Write?* Auckland, New Zealand: Heinemann Educational Books, 1975. Clay's work provides examples and rationale for encouraging early writing. Numerous examples add to the effectiveness of her explanations of the learning-to-write process. Must reading for teachers of preschoolers and beginning writers and readers!

CRAMER, RONALD L. *Writing, Reading, and Language Growth.* Columbus, Ohio: Charles E. Merrill, 1978. Throughout Cramer's book are both examples of and suggestions for developing children's writing. One chapter is devoted entirely to ideas for writing.

GRAVES, DONALD H. "An Examination of the Writing Processes of Seven-Year-Old Children," *Research in the Teaching of English* 9 (Winter 1975): 227–241. This research report on writing behavior uses a case study analysis in addition to a comparison of writing in formal and informal classrooms.

_____. "Research Update: What Children Show Us about Revision," *Language Arts* 56 (March 1979): 312–319. This preliminary report of the New Hampshire Writing Project reveals that primary grade children gradually use revision as they write although revision for beginners is minimal except for the natural stages of development that accompany invented spelling.

HENNINGS, DOROTHY GRANT, and GRANT, BARBARA M. *Content and Craft: Written Expression in the Elementary School.* Englewood Cliffs, N.J.: Prentice-Hall, 1973. This book gives specific ideas for children's writing and of the acquisition of the tools for clear written communication.

KING, MARTHA L., and RENTEL, VICTOR. "Toward a Theory of Early Writing Development," *Research in the Teaching of English* 13 (October 1979): 243–253. This review and interpretation of research examines the writing process and children's understanding of story structure and features.

KOCH, KENNETH. *Wishes, Lies, and Dreams.* New York: Vintage Books, Chelsea House, 1970. The examples of children's poetry present convincing evidence that children can write powerfully and expressively.

WALTER, NINA WILLIS. *Let Them Write Poetry.* New York: Holt, Rinehart & Winston, 1964. Walter's paperback book explores poetry writing from the kindergarten through high school. Examples of children's writing are included, and the examples for developing awareness of poetic expression, of imagery, and of word quality are particularly well described.

ZUTELL, JERRY. "Some Psycholinguistic Perspectives on Children's Spelling," *Language Arts* 55 (October 1978): 844–850. Zutell reviews some recent research on children's acquisition of spelling, pointing out that there is a systematic, predictable, developmental patterning to children's seemingly erroneous spelling. He also gives guidelines for evaluating children's spelling.

5

Vocabulary Development in the Language Experience Approach

"What are words?
Words are how what you think inside comes out
And how to remember what you might forget about."[1]

To say we speak, listen, read, and write with words seems to be stating an all too obvious fact. Even so, is it not also essential to provide planned experiences for developing children's facility with words? To give experience form and substance, children need tools or words for translating events into language. A command of vocabulary is a necessity for conveying and receiving thoughts, feelings, and emotions. If children are to be equipped to put their thoughts into speech or writing and to understand the thoughts of speakers and authors, they must be equipped with the word knowledge these language tasks require.

Extending children's vocabulary is a major point of teaching communication in both spoken and written language. The goals of such instruction are to increase the stock of words used by students in their listening, speaking, reading, and writing, to promote awareness of fine shades of meaning, and to develop an attitude of interest in words. Applegate shows the results of these goals in an anecdote about a fourth grader who told his teacher, "Why, we don't have to be just *mad* anymore. We've learned new words, and now we can be *angry, frustrated, irritated,* or *furious.*[2]

Word knowledge is a significant factor in reading comprehension, while a limited vocabulary is an obstacle.[3] The more extensive a child's oral vocabulary, the greater his resources for associating meaning with printed words. Davis reports that one major obligation in teaching comprehension is to make pupils familiar with the meanings of as many words as possible.[4] However, word study should be done in meaningful context within sentence patterns. The language experience approach provides this.

In building children's vocabularies, attention must be directed to increasing each of the four types of vocabulary (listening, speaking, reading, and writing). Increased understanding of words in one facet of the language arts should add to understanding in the other facets. In fact, the language experience approach, with the expressive and receptive facets of language, provides experiences that contribute to vocabulary development in all areas.

A basic distinction of vocabulary study in this approach is that *the study stems from children's oral and written language.* In other words, instead of starting with a list of words or passages from language arts textbooks as examples for study, the words selected originate in the children's speech, stories, and word banks. Word power will grow as children encounter situations in which they need to communicate. In word study, as in all aspects of language experience learning, practical application is the base from which language develops. John Holt states that, "What we have to recognize is . . . that it is the effort to use words well, to say what he wants to say, to people whom he trusts, and wants to reach and move, that alone will teach a young person to use words better."[5]

Research supports the importance of personal meaning and motivation in vocabulary learning. Olson and Pau find that children require significantly fewer trials to learn highly emotional words than are required to learn words without strong emotional associations.[6]

Sylvia Ashton-Warner who achieved phenomenal success in working with Maori children of New Zealand calls her work with reading vocabulary "key vocabulary" as she makes use of personal word files. She communicates the necessity for personal involvement in the learning as she describes the child who stalled for months on the words *come, look, and* and then learned *police, butcher knife, kill, gaol, hand,* and *fire engine* in four minutes in response to the question of what he was afraid of.[7] The words he *wanted to learn* were used to teach him to read. The high impact of the language experience content can affect the learning of reading vocabulary and thus offset the lack of systematic repetition.

Henderson, Estes, and Stonecash report that children instructed in a language experience approach do acquire sight vocabulary and that the number of words learned compares favorably with the words introduced in

69

basal readers.[8] These researchers also report that the high frequency function words of the language were frequently present in children's word banks.

Constant extension of the reading vocabulary is a goal of all reading programs at all levels. Language experience reading programs must give attention to a reading vocabulary, although the materials lack a controlled vocabulary. Because of the lack of vocabulary control and repetition, teachers may be concerned about students learning a reading vocabulary. In her review of research on the language experience approach, Hall refutes the often stated reservation that language experience programs may neglect vocabulary learning.[9] The use of word banks can provide much of the repetition for vocabulary learning in the beginning stages of instruction.

In the first stages of instruction children are exposed to all the written vocabulary used in experience stories. However, teachers should not expect that all words written in any story will be learned by those who have participated in creating and reading that story. Each child will identify the words she can read, and those words will go into the individual word bank. In other words, from the first experience stories children will identify one, two, or several words. Gradually, the stock of words known will increase. Also, some children with a month or two of instruction can identify all the words in the experience stories in their individual folders, even though at the time those stories were written, they could only identify two or three words in each story.

Concepts Children Need to Learn about Words

Not only should children use language effectively with ever-increasing vocabularies, but they should also know how words convey meaning in our language. The following list identifies some basic concepts which should be developed with elementary children.

1. *The word is a unit of meaning in the language.* Since word units are obviously distinct to adults, it is often assumed that the word units are equally distinct to children. Research studies of beginning readers' concept of a word have shown that this concept is not clear to the beginning reader.[10,11] Rystrom notes, "It seems likely that children do not learn what a word is until they have learned to read."[12] In the prereading and beginning reading stages, the concept of word can be shown functionally with language experience stories. (See p. 108.)

2. *Words help express our thoughts.* In order to develop vocabulary as well as any language skill, pupils must see the

need for communication in useful settings. Word study should help children understand the interrelationships of speaking, listening, reading, and writing. Pupils should discover that the words they speak can be written and read. They should discover, too, that the words of others can be written and spoken.

3. *The exact meaning of a word is dependent upon the use of the words in context.* Vocabulary study must be in connection with the language patterns in which the words occur. Lefevre believes that the sentence, not the word, is the smallest unit of meaning in our language.[13] Goodman puts immense stress on the importance of the syntactical system in reading as he states, "The meaning of a sentence depends on the words or morphemes that compose it, but it is always more than the sum of their meanings."[14] Word study must deal with words used in contextual settings. As children discuss multiple meanings, it is easy to show that the exact meaning of a word cannot be determined without its context. Developing an awareness of fine shades of meaning and selecting the most appropriate word for the meaning intended must be fostered.

4. *The specific function of a word is determined by the syntactic patterning of language.* Often the words that are most difficult for the beginner or remedial reader are the structure words of the language, such as *of, what, was,* and *on,* which lack any concrete referent and must be understood in the context of a sentence if meaning is to be connected with these words. These basic words occur frequently in language experience products just as they occur frequently in all language use. Instead of isolated drill or considerable practice on these words, children should use them through the reading and writing of language experience materials. Activities with sentence building and the discussion of sentences used in children's writing can illustrate language structure and word functions in sentence patterns. Having children label parts of speech or the formal word classifications of English is not the purpose of vocabulary teaching. Instead, the objective is effective use of vocabulary for the reception and expression of ideas.

5. Some meanings can be expressed by more than one word. Children should be alerted to synonyms as one means of increasing word power. As children work with their individual word boxes and as a group compiles class word banks, there will be many examples of synonyms. Modified cloze activities can also help to extend vocabulary learning using synonyms.

Types of Vocabulary

In discussing children's vocabularies, it is again necessary to look at the four dimensions of the language arts (listening, speaking, reading, and writing). Children have more than one type of vocabulary, and teachers must be concerned with the development of each type. A child's listening vocabulary is those words he can understand when others use them, although he may not use them in his own speech or recognize them in print. A child has a speaking vocabulary composed of those words which he uses in his speech. As a child learns to read, he acquires a reading vocabulary composed of those words that he can recognize in printed form and with which he can associate a meaning. As a child learns to write and spell, he acquires a writing vocabulary. In the early elementary years, the listening vocabulary is the largest, the speaking vocabulary is next, then reading, then the writing vocabulary last. However, the reading vocabulary may surpass the speaking vocabulary in the intermediate grades for those children progressing well in reading.

In the language experience approach, the four vocabularies are extended through activities with group and individual word banks, literature experiences, and writing and speaking activities. In the elementary school, concern with reading and writing has overshadowed the teaching of listening and speaking. In vocabulary instruction, stress must be placed on listening and speaking as well as on written language.

Individual Word Banks

Word banks or files kept by individual pupils are one of the major materials in the language experience approach. An individual word bank is a personal vocabulary file kept by each pupil and used in many ways for promoting vocabulary development and language awareness. A word is put into the bank after it has been used in an oral or written sentence pattern and after a child is able to read it. In the initial stages of reading instruction, the word banks are used primarily to reinforce the learning of reading vocabulary. As children progress in reading skills, they can use individual word banks as a reference for spelling and writing activities and for discussions about words. In this section, the word banks will be discussed first in relation to beginning reading instruction and then to other types of language study.

Functions

The major functions of the individual word banks are

1. To serve as a record of the reading vocabulary of individual students,

2. To serve as references for creative writing and spelling,
3. To provide reinforcement through repeated exposure to words,
4. To serve as stimulus words for examples for skill instruction,
5. To provide independent activities with word games, matching activities, sentence building, and
6. To provide examples for group language study.

Starting Word Banks

Teachers frequently ask, "How is a word bank started?" "What format is the most practical?" "How can words be classified?" "How can the word banks be used for independent activities?" "How can the word banks be used for directed language study?" The simplest way of starting individual word banks with a class is with a group or a personal experience story. Any word that a child can identify can be written for his word bank. For example, if the class has composed a group story about the classroom pet, a hamster, one child may be able to read the words *hamster* and *brown*. If so, these words will be placed on cards for his word bank. Another child may be able to read the words *hamster, little,* and *eat.* These three words are written for this child's word file. Each child will choose different words, and the teacher should not attempt to have a group of pupils select identical words for mastery.

The above procedure can be followed when working with individual experience stories. The child may be asked to underline the words in his story which he knows. Again, these words are written on cards for his word bank. These words cards will be used for many of the activities described later in this chapter.

Other procedures may be used for starting or adding to the individual word banks. At first, pupils' names can be used to arouse curiosity about words. The first word in a child's bank could be his name. As pupils learn to read the names of their classmates, these words could be included in the word banks. Pupils may learn some words from signs and from bulletin board captions around the room. The teacher can explain to the group that if they can read those words, cards will be placed in their banks.

Another source for starting or for adding to the word banks is children's literature. After reading a story to the class, the teacher may ask, "What was the most interesting word you heard in this story?" or "What word in the story would you like to know?" One variation of the interesting word idea was used in the compilation of a picture dictionary with a remedial group who selected words for the dictionary from literature examples. After hearing the story *The Tenth Good Thing about Barney,*[15] the group selected *fertilizer* and *destination* as words to be included. Typically, children are intrigued by words they consider different and ones they think adults may think they won't know.

73

Some Cautions

Some cautions should be noted regarding the above procedures. The teacher should not be in a hurry to have children add too many words to the banks since this may lead to confusion. The rate of learning will differ from pupil to pupil, and the purpose of word banks should not be viewed by pupils as collecting as many words as possible.

Opportunities for rereading and for repeated exposure to words should be provided, especially in the initial stages of instruction. Teachers should not be upset when children occasionally forget a word. In working with commercial materials, children will also forget words. Reteaching is in order in both cases. In the language experience approach, reteaching or extra practice can be provided by having the child find the sentence in the story in which she first used the word and by having her read the sentence and underline the word. The child can talk about the meaning of the word and match the card from the bank to the word in the story. One category of words in a bank can be "Words I Need to Work On," and a missed word can be placed in this category. The child can be directed to build a sentence using the forgotten word with cards from the word bank.

Another caution regarding the word banks relates to the selection of words. Children, not the teacher, should select the words they wish to know. However, with some student-composed materials the teacher may ask, "Do you know this word? It is a word you will use in many stories." Some teacher suggestions may be offered, but the selection of the words in the individual word banks remains the child's choice.

Another caution is not to isolate words from context. The bank words were originally introduced in context, and the follow-up activities should also be related to context. Many teachers write a sentence or phrase on each word card as it is placed in a word bank collection. The vocabulary work should never consist of flash card drill, since such an activity is a nonreading situation without context.

Group Word Banks

Word banks can be developed with an entire class or with subgroups within a class. Generally in most classes, there will be many group banks for various categories of word study. With the group word banks greater attention is placed on general language development and less on reading vocabulary in contrast with individual word banks.

Functions

The functions of the group word banks are

1. To develop language awareness and interest in word study,
2. To focus language study on word categories and functions,
3. To serve as a reference (a type of class dictionary) for word study or as a spelling check when doing independent writing, and
4. To provide materials for independent activities with words.

Starting Word Banks

In developing group word banks, discussions and group experience stories will be the main source. The easiest way to start group banks with any class is to discuss word categories such as colors, animals, and naming words. For example, in kindergarten or first grade, the first group word file could be an outgrowth of a group experience story. If the pupils have written a story about the colors of the fall leaves, they could be asked to find all the words that name colors. These words could then be written on cards and placed in a box or envelope labeled "color words." If the children have written some chart stories about animals, they could reread these stories and find all the words that name animals and include this classification in a word file. Numerous categories can and should be used.

Word meanings in the group files should be familiar to pupils, and the words added to the banks should have been used in a contextual setting in the talk and writing of the class. The cards for the group banks can include a sentence definition or a picture with each word. Teachers may wish to number the group experience stories and have a folder of typed copies, available in the classroom writing or reading center. This folder should include an envelope of word bank cards, which are numbered according to the story in which the words were used. This folder can be useful for independent activities and as a reference for word study.

No single format is satisfactory to all teachers. Regardless of the arrangement, the bank should permit easy reclassification of words by students. Having each word on a separate card or slip of paper is recommended. A notebook type of listing does not have the feature of easy manipulation or reclassification. Teachers generally find that oak tag or other relatively heavy paper increases the durability of the word cards. Many teachers find that index cards are easy to use and to file in either a standard size file box or in cardboard boxes.

A card of $1'' \times 2''$ is generally adequate for individual use, especially if pupils are going to build sentences at their desks. Also, a small card is more satisfactory for comparison with a word in an individual experience

75

story. During the beginning stages, a teacher may prefer using large word cards and shoe boxes for files.

Providing envelopes for classification into such categories as suggested previously is helpful. Many ways of classifying words should be used and changed throughout the school year.

The group word banks may utilize 4" × 6" or 6" × 8" index cards for visibility by the total group. These can be kept in shoe boxes or large file boxes in the writing center. Again, envelopes for classification are useful, and as the files expand beyond the first grade level, a separate box can be used for each category. For example, there may be banks of synonyms, antonyms, words with multiple meanings, descriptive words, and interesting language expressions, word pictures, and similes or metaphors.

Activities with Word Banks

An advantage of the word banks for language study is their adaptability to many activities. The classification activity, which is one of the most valuable, can begin very early in the reading and language arts instruction by varying the level and categories according to the children's maturity. Perhaps the simplest means of classification is by alphabetical order. While this is a useful and practical means of locating words easily, the classification of words should not be limited to filing entries in alphabetical order. Language study will be much more appropriate if children study word qualities, definitions, and functions.

As an example of introducing the classification of words at the beginning reading level, a teacher could ask a small group of children to bring their word banks to the reading table and find words that name things such as people, food, or animals. Another time children could be directed to find all the words that are action or descriptive words. The labeling of nouns, verbs, and other parts of speech is unimportant. What is important is that the children understand how words function in a sentence context to convey meaning and that children constantly increase their word power.

Word banks can lead to the discussion of word categories and then to the development of each category. The teacher can ask the pupils to find the most interesting words in their banks and tell why a particular word is interesting to them. In one first grade class, a child volunteered *glitter* and *sparkle* as the most interesting words. These words had been used in a story describing a Halloween costume. Another child said that *diesel engine* and *blast-off* were the most interesting words. The practice of identifying interesting words can contribute considerably to language awareness.

Children will be introducing to many classifications as they progress in reading, and teachers will find word banks extremely useful for working with multiple meanings, synonyms, antonyms, and homonyms. A classification for a particular word should change as the children realize that a particular word may fit in a number of categories depending upon its use in context.

Word banks can be used for sentence building activities as a child or a group of children combine the words in different patterns. The word banks can provide the basis for work with kernel sentences and their extension with additional words. For example, two words such as *Boy jumped* or *Cat ate* can be selected from a bank, and the children can be asked to find words that might describe the boy or the cat, words which tell how the boy jumped or what the cat ate. Children can select two words for kernel sentences and ask their classmates to add to the original sentence. When this activity uses the word banks, children are working with *their* language as they extend their knowledge of how words function in sentence patterns.

Word banks are practical for independent reading and language activities in classroom writing centers, described in chapter 9. Children can work in pairs or teams as they read each other's words and stories or as they build sentences with the word cards. Some children may want to compile individual dictionaries by writing definitions for the words in their banks.

This student uses descriptive words from her word bank to practice vocabulary development.

Children should be encouraged to refer to both the individual and group word banks when doing creative writing. Writing can be motivated by having children select words from the bank to make an interesting title, and then they can write a story for that title. When studying word categories, children could write a story using as many words of a particular category as possible.

A sample of frequently used topics for group word banks includes the following:

Descriptive words	Compound words
Naming words	Words with prefixes
Action words	Words with suffixes
Words for food	Rhyming words
Interesting words	Synonyms
Words for sounds	Homonyms
Words for said	Science words
Words for colors	Opposites
Words for people	Words with more than one
Words for animals	meaning
Sports words	Three-syllable words
Words for feelings	Four-syllable words

The first column appears more interesting than the second, which is concerned with content often labeled as "skill-centered."

Other Activities for Word Study

Pupils in the intermediate grades can extend and deepen their study for words by probing into the origins of words. Perhaps the class can keep banks for words with interesting origins. Dictionary study can be helpful with this activity as students are alerted to the information about word origins to be found in a dictionary. The brief pamphlet *Pageant of Words*[16] has a number of suggestions for studying word origins and includes the names of appropriate trade books related to word study.

In Other Words is the title of both a beginning and an intermediate thesaurus designed for elementary students.[17,18] These two books can be valuable for developing children's vocabularies as well as adding to their interest in words.

A notebook could be kept on the writing center table or in the reading center for pupil use in recording interesting words found in their independent reading. They can also keep personal lists of these words.

Activities with literature and creative writing also promote vocabulary growth, and the reader is directed to chapter 4 and 6 for other ideas relating to vocabulary.

Summary

78

Increasing children's listening, speaking, reading, and writing vocabularies receives major attention in the language experience approach. Opportunities to use words in personal communication situations in speaking and writing provide an excellent means for developing word power. In this approach, many opportunities for discussion of words will occur, and developing an awareness of words should be a continuing goal. In vocabulary development, as in other concerns in this approach, the three characteristics of pupil-composed materials, the interrelationships of all the language arts, and the lack of vocabulary control are apparent.

Through language experience activities children should discover many ways of using words for communication. Individual and group word banks constitute a major tool for vocabulary study as they are used as a record of words learned and as materials for numerous other activities. The teacher's responsibility is to provide the setting and the stimuli for word study growing from the child's own language and from the communication activities of the classroom.

NOTES

1. From Paul Rand and Ann Rand, *Sparkle and Spin* (New York: Harcourt Brace Jovanovich, Inc., 1957).

2. Mauree Applegate, *Easy in English* (Evanston, Ill.: Row, Peterson and Company, 1962), p. 29.

3. Frederick Davis, "Research in Comprehension in Reading," *Reading Research Quarterly* 3 (Summer 1968):508.

4. Davis, "Research in Comprehension in Reading," p. 543.

5. John Holt, "Introduction" in Herbert Kohl, *Teaching the "Unteachable"* (New York: The New York Review, 1966), p. 9.

6. David R. Olson and A. S. Pau, "Emotionally Loaded Words and the Acqusition of a Sight Vocabulary," *Journal of Educational Psychology* 57 (June 1966):174–78.

7. Sylvia Ashton-Warner, *Teacher* (New York: Simon & Schuster, 1963), p. 43.

8. Edmund H. Henderson, Thomas H. Estes, and Susan Stonecash, "An Exploratory Study of Word Acquisition among First-Graders at Midyear in a Language Experience Approach," *Journal of Reading Behavior* 4 (Summer 1972):28.

9. MaryAnne Hall, *The Language Experience Approach for Teaching Reading: A Research Perspective* (Newark, Del.: International Reading Association, 1978), pp. 27–28.

10. John Downing, "How Children Think about Reading," *The Reading Teacher* 23 (December 1969):217–30.

11. Nancy J. Meltzer and Robert Herse. "The Boundaries of Written Words as Seen by First Graders," *Journal of Reading Behavior* 1 (Summer 1969):32–40.

12. Richard Rystrom, "Linguistics and the Teaching of Reading," *Journal of Reading Behavior* 4 (Winter 1972):37

13. Carl A. Lefevre, *Linguistics and the Teaching of Reading* (New York: McGraw-Hill, 1964), p. 6.

14. Kenneth S. Goodman, "Words and Morphemes in Reading," in *Psycholinguistics and the Teaching of Reading,* eds. Kenneth S. Goodman and James T. Fleming (Newark, Del.: International Reading Association, 1969), p. 27.

15. Judith Viorst, *The Tenth Good Thing about Barney* (New York: Atheneum, 1971).

16. *Pageant of Words* (Glenview, Ill.: Scott, Foresman and Company, 1966).

17. W. Cabell Greet, William A. Jenkins, and Andrew Schiller, *In Other Words: A Beginning Thesaurus* (Glenview, Ill.: Scott, Foresman and Company, 1978).

18. W. Cabell Greet, William A Jenkins, and Andrew Schiller, *In Other Words: A Junior Thesaurus* (Glenview, Ill.: Scott, Foresman and Company, 1978).

Suggested Readings

APPLEGATE, MAUREE. *Easy in English.* Evanston, Ill.: Row, Peterson and Company, 1962, chapter 2. Applegate conveys the message of the chapter title, "Words Make the Difference" perceptively and includes activities for extending vocabulary in creative ways.

ASHTON-WARNER, SYLVIA. *Teacher.* New York: Simon & Schuster, Inc., 1963. The description of the "key vocabulary" in teaching reading shows the use of individual word files for vocabulary. The reader will note the emotional impact of the words selected by Mrs. Ashton-Warner's pupils.

GLAUS, MARLENE. *From Thoughts to Words.* Champaign, Ill.: National Council of Teachers of English, 1965. This paperback book is a collection of ideas for the classroom teacher who wants to combine creativity and language expression.

GROFF, PATRICK. "The Topsy Turvy World of 'Sight' Words," *The Reading Teacher* 27 (March 1974): 572–578. As the title indicates, the author attempts to clarify definitions of reading vocabulary and to present research results related to vocabulary learning.

HALL, MARYANNE; RIBOVICH, JERILYN K.; and RAMIG, CHRISTOPHER J. *Reading and the Elementary School Child.* New York: Van Nostrand, 1979. Chapters 4, 5, and 6 include discussions of the teaching of reading vocabulary from beginning reading through the upper elementary levels.

JOHNSON, DALE D., and PEARSON, P. DAVID. *Teaching Reading Vocabulary.* New York: Holt, Rinehart & Winston, 1978. This book includes some imaginative ways for expanding children's vocabularies. The section on the use of the thesaurus in chapter 7 is particularly helpful.

6

LITERATURE AS A LANGUAGE EXPERIENCE

Literature as a language experience presents opportunities for developing children's language facility in personal, communicative, creative, and functional ways. The place of literature in an elementary reading program is generally accepted as being important in promoting pleasurable experiences with reading, thereby contributing to the development of a permanent interest in and favorable attitudes toward reading. The values of literature for entertainment, extending experience backgrounds, and developing understanding of self and others have been discussed by many authorities on children's literature.[1,2,3] However, the contribution of literature as a language enriching experience needs greater attention than it currently receives in many classrooms. The freshness and originality of language in children's literature is one of its unique qualities that no other materials or curriculum experiences can offer.

Literature is a *personal* language experience since children respond to stories in individual ways and express their reactions to characters, plots, and themes in terms of their individual backgrounds. In encouraging divergent reactions to stories read to children and to those which they read for themselves, questions such as, "How did *you* feel?" "What would *you* have done?'' ''What did this story make *you* think of?'' will permit and encourage a variety of responses.

Literature is a *communicative* language experience because children use listening and reading to absorb ideas. As children respond thoughtfully and affectively to literature through listening, discussing, dramatizing, and writing, communication is promoted.

Literature is a *creative* language experience when it serves as a stimulus for creative thinking, leads to the writing of creative stories and poems, and provides the ideas for spontaneous drama.

Literature is a *functional* language experience as children see a purpose to activities with literature of high interest and meaningful content. The creative, personal, and communicative attributes contribute to the purposefulness of the literature experiences.

The value of literature in enriching language backgrounds is supported by Carol Chomsky's research.[4] In a study of children's linguistic development, she finds that for children who have been read to and/or who have read independently the stage of linguistic development is higher than for children who have not had the exposure to literature. Fasick reports that preschoolers' literature materials use a far wider range of syntactic patterns than do children's television programs.[5] She advocates the use of literature for development of children's language readiness.

This chapter expresses the interrelatedness of language experiences and literature. At all levels in the elementary school, there is a place for experiences with literature which expand vocabulary, build awareness of writing styles, and stimulate creative writing. Throughout the chapter, books are cited which are especially applicable in relating literature to other language experiences. The reader will also note that in the chapters on vocabulary development and creative writing references are also made to literature.

The Teacher's Role

The teacher must provide the time, the motivation, and the materials for children to explore the possibilities of developing language awareness through literature. In a study of children's reading preferences and habits, Helen Huus finds that the adults in the environment are a significant factor affecting interest in reading.[6] As the significant adult in the school environment, the teacher must provide the model of valuing literature.

In another source, Hall comments,

> With the growth of school libraries, the inclusion of librarians as part of elementary school faculties, and the increase in the quantity of books available on a range of levels and interests, teachers have more resources than ever before on which to draw in developing dynamic literature programs. However, the resources themselves cannot

produce excellent reading programs; teachers must actively draw upon these resources as they put a program into operation.[7]

A survey of the literature experiences provided by cooperating teachers who were working with student teachers shows that the experiences with literature in many classrooms were limited indeed.[8] Creative experiences were particularly sparse.

Experiences with literature are essential in any good reading program, and in all classrooms the following activities and facilities should be included:

1. The daily reading aloud of a children's literature selection by the teacher
2. A classroom library corner or table where books are displayed attractively and changed frequently
3. Opportunities for children to explore books as an independent activity
4. Regularly scheduled time for independent reading
5. Opportunities for individuals to use the school library as needed, by having open access to it as well as having regularly scheduled library periods
6. Creative activities related to literature (art, drama, creative writing)

In addition, the teacher must offer activities with literature that contribute directly to the language experience reading program. However, the major purpose in reading literature to children and in encouraging personal reading is to have them enjoy stories. Never should the enjoyment be overlooked as literature is used to contribute to the total language program in some of the ways discussed in this chapter. However, it cannot be assumed that children will become aware of writing styles or of the creative use of language without some direct guidance by the teacher.

The teacher must know many books, develop some techniques for alerting children to language through literature, and provide opportunities for children to use models from literature to express their own ideas in spoken and written language.

LITERATURE AND LANGUAGE AWARENESS

Language quality is one of the hallmarks of good literature. One of the reasons literature belongs in the elementary curriculum is simply because it is *imaginative language.* Jacobs talks about "colorful, tongue-tickling words and

83

neatly turned phrases" which are a part of storytelling.[9] Through literature, children can experience creative uses of language in a very natural, informal way. It is hoped that through exposure to the language of literature children will add to their ability to expressively use language. Exposure to models of original and creative expression by gifted authors is essential if real language awareness and power is to develop in the elementary years. In using literature with children, the intent is for them to hear and read the best that has been written and to express their own thoughts and ideas. During the early school years when children's reading skills are minimal, hearing literature read is their major exposure to the imaginative use of language. Blatt identifies children's literature selections that contribute to a sense of language awareness through a number of language arts activities.[10] The language collection activities suggested later in this chapter will extend language awareness.

Although children will have more experiences with prose literature than with poetry, poetry also can stimulate language awareness and creative responses in children. Imagery, figurative language, and brevity of thought can add to the appeal of this branch of literature. Interest, enjoyment, appreciation, and a love for poetry can be nurtured by reading many examples aloud. Teachers should be familiar with anthologies and should develop personal anthologies of their own favorites. They can help build an awareness of mood, visual and auditory imagery, and emotional responses through poetry. In the following sections on creative writing, vocabulary development, and author's style, examples are drawn from both prose and poetry. The same methodology can be used with each.

LITERATURE ANd
WRITTEN EXPRESSION

One of the major applications of literature in the total language curriculum is written expression. Through the awareness of language, development of vocabulary, and understanding of style, the tools for personal writing are acquired.

If children are expected to write creatively, they should be exposed to creative writing of other authors. The input of ideas through literature is vital if children are going to have a reservoir of knowledge and structures for their own creativity. As pupils hear and read models of prose and poetry, they can be stimulated to write their own stories and poems. For example, fables, tall tales, and haiku are excellent models. Examples of haiku poetry can be found in *Cricket Songs,* by Harry Behn,[11] and *In a Spring Garden,* by Richard Lewis.[12] In haiku poetry the seventeen syllable form can be discussed, but attention should be given to the thoughts expressed instead of to the number of syllables included. As in all creative writing, the thought is more important than the form.

Children can share independent reading with others through writing. Although written book reports of a routine type are not in harmony with the philosophy of the language experience approach, certain types of writing about books should be encouraged. Children can be introduced to book reviews through newspapers and periodicals and should experiment with this style of writing. Children can try writing personal reviews of their favorite books. These reviews can be featured in the class newspaper or displayed in the classroom reading corner. Children can write about or to their favorite authors and share these writings in small interest groups and with members of other classes. Character sketches and descriptions for book jackets are other types of writing about books.

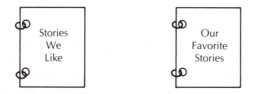

In each type of writing, the teacher first introduces a model to the children. For example, when students write book jacket descriptions, the teacher could read the blurbs from several familiar jackets to them, and the class could compose a description for another jacket. Then the children could write individual blurbs to interest other children in books.

A book written and illustrated by a group of classmates is intriguing to this student.

For young children, literature can lead to the creation of group experience charts, individual experience stories, and group books as discussed in chapter 3. After hearing a story read aloud, children as a group can dictate their reactions to it or write a summary of the plot. A chart could be made to interest another class in a book, or a group book of these reactions could be made. For example, if children listen to *Swimmy,* by Leo Lionni,[13] they could write stories about fish; or after hearing *Rufus,* by Tomi Ungerer,[14] they could dictate stories about bats. Among the other easy picture-story books that children enjoy are *Harry, the Dirty Dog,*[15] and the other Harry books by Gene Zion; *Crictor,*[16] by Tomi Ungerer; *Danny the Dinosaur*[17] and *Sammy the Seal,*[18] by Syd Hoff; *Lyle, Lyle, Crocodile,*[19] by Bernard Waber.

Writing stemming from books can become increasingly complex as children move into the intermediate grades. Features of plot structure, characterization, descriptive language, and dialogue can be shown through reading literature models followed by discussion of particular features, and ending with children writing to show a particular quality or technique. A very informative source for detailed descriptions of how to show how literature models to lead to personal writing is Stewig's book, *Read to Write.*[20]

Literature and Writing Styles

Style is the quality that makes a piece of writing distinctive and individual. Arbuthnot describes style as ". . . difficult to define, a quality of which children are unconscious and yet one to which they respond as surely as they respond to a smile."[21] Exposing children to various writing styles in literature encourages adapting language to their ideas and helps them use language more effectively. Continued contact with literature develops ever increasing sensitivity to language. As children examine writing styles, they should be alerted to certain techniques used by writers. The introduction to these techniques can best be illustrated by their occurrence in literature. Studying authors' styles should be carried over to pupils' writing experiences using different moods or techniques.

In alerting children to the mood of stories, the teacher can read serious and light stories on the same topic to the children for contrast. Children can also identify the words used by an author to create a certain mood. For example, children could compare the mystical mood in *Where Does the Butterfly Go When It Rains?,* by May Garelick,[22] with the factual descriptions in *Rain Drop Splash,* by Alvin Tresselt.[23] Children in upper grades can discuss the differences in mood between various books read in their independent study. Comparative reading experiences such as those discussed by Smith and Barrett can heighten appreciation of variation in style.[24] Among their suggestions is for middle grade students to compare biographies of the same individual written by different authors.

Petty and Bowen identify personification, onomatopoeia, alliteration, and internal rhyme as devices that can be easily learned and applied by elementary pupils.[25] Children need not learn the technical names for these techniques but should recognize them in literature and use them in their writing.

Personification can be pointed out to young children as they recognize the human characteristics attributed to inanimate objects in stories like *Mike Mulligan and His Steam Shovel*,[26] and *The Little House*,[27] both by Virginia Burton, and *Little Toot*,[28] *Loopy*,[29] and *Hercules*,[30] by Hardy Gramatky. Many other examples of personification exist in children's literature selections. Pupils can be asked to write stories using personification.

In a clinic situation with remedial readers, the grab bag technique has been used to have children experiment with personification. A number of objects are placed in the grab bag, and the children are asked to pick one and then write a story beginning with "I am. . . ." Teachers can ask children to compose a story with an object as the main character.

As appropriate examples occur in the poetry read to children, the teacher may comment on the auditory qualities that make particular poems distinctive. Comments such as, "When you write a poem, you might want to use several words which begin alike in a line," or "You might want to try to find words which sound like the idea the word represents," are good examples.

The concern is not to develop set techniques or styles for pupils but, through exposure and discussion, to have children realize that style changes according to content, purpose, mood, and author. Children should grasp the concept that different authors have different styles just as in class they have different styles. Teachers can encourage children to experiment in their writing by accepting their language, by giving them opportunities to discuss styles of writing in literature examples, and by providing situations for them to employ different styles and techniques in their personal writing.

LITERATURE AND VOCABULARY DEVELOPMENT

The fact that continued exposure to the language of others results in the development of speaking vocabulary is well documented by studies of the acquisition of oral language in the young child as he learns to speak from hearing the language of those in his environment. Exposure to the words of literature also adds to a child's vocabulary development. However, in addition to the informal exposure offered by literature, some steps can be taken by teachers to alert children to new words or interesting language descriptions. Teachers must seek to reinforce the informal exposure and to consciously build language awareness.

TECHNIQUES FOR PROMOTING VOCABULARY

A chart of interesting words, descriptive phrases, and word pictures from literature can be kept. The teacher must initiate the discussion of language

87

usage if awareness of language is to ensue. Books provide one of the best sources for stretching the imagination and expanding vocabulary. As children hear new stories and poems, they have an opportunity for adding new words to their listening and speaking vocabularies. The teacher's responsibility is to alert children before a story is read to listen for the interesting way an author describes a particular person or object, for all the words that describe a person's action, or for all the words that describe sounds.

A chart such as the following could be kept:

Interesting Language from Books

from *Listen, Rabbit**   "the rain was weeping down the eye of the window pane"

Word Pictures

from *Swimmy†*   "a lobster who moved about like a water moving machine"

---

*Aileen Fisher, *Listen, Rabbit* (New York: Crowell Collier & Macmillan, 1965).
†Lionni, *Swimmy*.

After reading a story to children, a teacher may ask, "What did you notice about the word _____ ?" "What did it mean?" "How did the author use that word?" "Do you know any other words which he could have used which mean the same thing?" (It is better not to interrupt a story to explain a word or concept; explanations should occur either before or after the reading.) The teacher may ask, "What was the most interesting or new word you heard in that story?" When one first grader was asked this question after listening to *The Camel Who Took a Walk* by Jack Tworkov,[31] he replied, "Flabbergasted." The teacher can ask, "What kind of person was _____ ?" or "How did _____ feel when _____ ?" Words such as *greedy, selfish, troublesome, frightened, unpleasant, understanding, sympathetic*, and *optimistic* might be discussed and added to the class word banks. A notebook could be kept on the writing center table or in the reading center for additional examples from independent reading.

Awareness of similes and metaphors begins even while children are in the prereading stage as they hear stories read aloud. The book *Swimmy* contains many examples of the interesting use of language through comparisons. Children can listen for how the lobster moved ("like a water-moving machine") or how the underwater flowers, the sea anemones, looked ("like pink palm trees swaying in the wind").[32] *The Sun Is a Golden Earring,*[33] mentioned in chapter 4, contains excellent examples of similes and metaphors. This terminology is unimportant for children in the elementary level. However, the ability to use comparisons to communicate clearly, imaginatively, and expressively must be developed. The poem "Cliche," in *It Doesn't Always Have to Rhyme* by Eve Merriam,[34] is excellent for having pupils identify comparisons. Children can extend the poem's idea to their own writing as they work with, "As warm as _____ ; as quiet as _____ ; as soft as _____ ; as quick as _____ ." Also, Alvin Tresselt's *How Far is Far,*[35] contains many imaginative descriptions that can be used to motivate children's writing.

Children's literature materials that are directly related to vocabulary study are *Sparkle and Spin,* by Ann and Paul Rand,[36] *Words, Words, Words,* by Mary O'Neill,[37] *A Hole Is to Dig,* by Ruth Krauss,[38] *Ounce, Dice, Trice,* by Alistair Reid,[39] and *A Riot of Quiet,* by Virginia Sicotte.[40]

SUMMARY

Children's literature plays an important part throughout the reading program. Trade books of many types should be used to enrich the language and experience backgrounds of the pupils. Books can help expand vocabularies, develop concepts, provide training in purposeful listening as well as develop the idea that reading is a pleasurable experience. Literature can add to a child's ability to use and understand language and express in words what he sees, hears, feels, thinks, and imagines. Literature models are an excellent source for motivating personal writing.

Literature is a language experience, but it is the teacher's responsibility to awaken the children's sensitivity to the language of literature. In so doing, the teacher must be aware of the examples of interesting language in children's books, must call the children's attention to these examples in a variety of ways, and must provide the stimulation and opportunities for children to develop their own creativity with language.

NOTES

1. May Hill Arbuthnot and Zena Sutherland, *Children and Books,* 4th ed. (Chicago: Scott, Foresman and Company, 1972).

2. Charlotte S. Huck, *Children's Literature in the Elementary School* (New York: Holt, Rinehart, & Winston, 1979).

3. Leland B. Jacobs, "Children's Experiences with Literature," in *Children, and the Language Arts,* ed. Virgil Herrick and Leland B. Jacobs (Englewood Cliffs, N.J.: Prentice-Hall, Inc., 1955), pp. 192–217.

4. Carol Chomsky, "Stages in Language Development and Reading Exposure," *Harvard Educational Review* 42 (February 1972): 1–33.

5. Adele M. Fasick, "Television Language and Book Language," *Elementary English* 50 (January 1973): 125–32.

6. Helen Huus, "Interpreting Research in Children's Literature," in *Children Books and Reading, Perspectives in Reading No. 3* (Newark, Del.: International Reading Association, 1964), p. 127.

89

7. MaryAnne Hall, "Literature Experiences Provided by Cooperating Teachers," *The Reading Teacher* 24 (February 1971): 431, 465.

8. Hall, "Literature Experiences Provided by Cooperating Teachers."

9. Jacobs, "Children's Experiences with Literature," p. 198.

10. Gloria Blatt, "Playing with Language," *The Reading Teacher* 31 (February 1978): 487–93.

11. Harry Behn, comp., *Cricket Songs* (New York: Harcourt, Brace & World, 1964).

12. Richard Lewis, comp., *In a Spring Garden* (New York: The Dial Press, 1965).

13. Leo Lionni, *Swimmy* (New York: Pantheon Books, 1963).

14. Tomi Ungerer, *Rufus* (New York: Harper & Row, 1961).

15. Gene Zion, *Harry, the Dirty Dog* (New York: Harper and Row, 1956).

16. Tomi Ungerer, *Crictor* (New York: Harper and Row, 1958).

17. Syd Hoff, *Danny the Dinosaur* (New York: Harper and Row, 1958).

18. Syd Hoff, *Sammy the Seal* (New York: Harper and Row, 1959).

19. Bernard Waber, *Lyle, Lyle, Crocodile* (Boston: Houghton Mifflin, 1965).

20. John W. Stewig, *Read to Write* (New York: Hawthorn Books, 1975).

21. May Hill Arbuthnot, *Children and Books,* 3d ed. (Chicago: Scott, Foresman and Company, 1964), p. 18.

22. May Garelick, *Where Does the Butterfly Go When It Rains?* (New York: William R. Scott, 1963).

23. Alvin Tresselt, *Rain Drop Splash* (New York: Lothrop, Lee & Shepard, 1946).

24. Richard J. Smith and Thomas C. Barrett, *Teaching Reading in the Middle Grades* (Reading, Mass.: Addison Wesley, 1979).

25. Walter T. Petty and Mary E. Bowen, *Slithery Snakes and Other Aids to Children's Writing* (New York: Appleton-Century-Crofts, 1967), pp. 64–70.

26. Virginia Burton, *Mike Mulligan and His Steam Shovel* (Boston: Houghton Mifflin, 1939).

27. Virginia Burton, *The Little House* (Boston: Houghton Mifflin, 1942).

28. Hardy Gramatky, *Little Toot* (New York: G. P. Putnam's Sons, 1939).

29. Hardy Gramatky, *Loopy* (New York: G. P. Putnam's Sons, 1939).

30. Hardy Gramatky, *Hercules* (New York: G. P. Putnam's Sons, 1940).

31. Jack Tworkov, *The Camel Who Took a Walk* (New York: E.P. Dutton & Co., 1951).

32. Lionni, *Swimmy.*

33. Natalia Belting. *The Sun Is a Golden Earring* (New York: Holt, Rinehart & Winston, 1962).

34. Eve Merriam, *It Doesn't Always Have to Rhyme* (New York: Atheneum, 1966).

35. Alvin Tresselt, *How Far Is Far?* (New York: Parents' Magazine Press, 1964).

36. Paul Rand and Ann Rand, *Sparkle and Spin* (New York: Harcourt Brace Jovanovich, 1957).

37. Mary O'Neill, *Words, Words, Words* (New York: Doubleday & Company, 1966).

38. Ruth Krauss, *A Hole Is to Dig* (New York: Harper & Row, 1952).

39. Alistair Reid, *Ounce, Dice, Trice* (Boston: Little, Brown and Company, 1958).

40. Virginia Sicotte, *A Riot of Quiet (New York: Holt, Rinehart & Winston, 1969).*

Suggested Readings

BLATT, GLORIA. "Playing with Language," *The Reading Teacher* 31 (February 1978): 487–493. An extensive bibliography is included to support Blatt's views that literature is a rich resource for encouraging language experimentation and extension.

HOPKINS, LEE BENNETT. *Books Are by People.* New York: Citation Press, 1969. Anecdotes and comments by 104 authors and illustrations of children's books form the substance of this unique publication. There is a sequel, *More Books by More People.*

HUCK, CHARLOTTE S. *Children's Literature in the Elementary School.* New York: Holt, Rinehart & Winston, 1979. Chapters 11, 12, and 13 are concerned with the planned experiences with literature in the elementary classroom and with projects children can execute related to their reading.

_____. "Literature as the Content of Reading," *Theory into Practice* 16 (December 1977): 363–371. Huck proposes that "real books" be the substance of reading programs as she elaborates on the values of literature.

STEWIG, JOHN WARREN. *Read to Write.* New York: Hawthorn Books, 1975. This book draws upon literature examples to provide models, features, and ideas both to motivate children to write and to help them understand the qualities of effective writing.

WHITEHEAD, ROBERT. *Children's Literature: Strategies of Teaching.* Englewood Cliffs, N.J.: Prentice-Hall, 1968. Many activities with children's books are described in this publication. Many of the ideas can correlate with language experiences as children talk and write about their personal reading. Chapter 5 deals specifically with oral and written experiences with literature.

7

Comprehension and Language Experience

Comprehension is, of course, the objective of reading, and language experience communication is certainly meaning centered. Language experience reading for beginners is very strong on meaning, yet the language experience approach has been criticized as inadequate for developing reading comprehension beyond the beginning stages. The point of view expressed here is that language experience instruction has much to offer in furthering comprehension through the active involvement of the learner in both producing and receiving messages through written language.

This chapter explores developing reading and language comprehension through language experience activities. Following a discussion of the nature of and factors affecting comprehension, attention is given to comprehension for the unproficient reader, to relationship of writing and comprehension, and to language experience activities that foster comprehension.

Comprehension Defined

Comprehension is defined here as the reconstruction of a message from print.[1] The process is a psycholinguistic one which requires the interaction of the reader's thoughts and language with the ideas represented in written language. As a reader understands, he must integrate the information from the reading selection with his existing knowledge (his schemata). In some situations he must reorganize his previous knowledge to accommodate the new concepts and ideas. Simons describes the comprehension process as "the mental operations which take place in the reader's head while he is reading. These operations are generally not observable and not open to introspection."[2]

Certainly, language experience learning features a match between the ideas of a reader and the instructional reading material, and this instruction values comprehension. Comprehension development must be done with meaningful whole language and does not come through isolated word and letter study, which is usually a nonreading and noncommunication situation.

Hall, Ribovich, and Ramig identify factors affecting comprehension in the following statement.

> Comprehension is influenced by a number of factors: the extensiveness of a reader's experiential background, his conceptual knowledge, and his language competence; the level of the reading material, language patterns, and vocabulary used, along with the concept load or density of the material; the reader's interest in and the relevancy of the content; and the quality of instruction, including the teacher's effectiveness in helping students set purposes for reading, selecting appropriate materials bridging the gap between the reader's background and the content of the reading material, and utilizing questioning strategies effectively.[3]

The factors related to the reader, the material, and the quality of instruction can be applied to examining comprehension in language experience learning. The match between learner and material is certainly evident in language experience. Through language experience activities, the language competence and conceptual and vocabulary background should be broadened, and quality instruction will extend reading comprehension through use of varied types of literature and varied types of writing to teach passage organization and story structure, as well as stressing the application of comprehension strategies in many language experience projects.

In a recently reported study based on classroom observations, Durkin finds that attention to comprehension is minimal.[4] In fact, she reports that less than one percent of the time devoted to reading is spent on direct instruction in comprehension. If the focus on comprehension in language experience is compared to that in basals, language experience may in reality offer more in comprehension than is evident in the implementation of the most commonly used instructional approach.

93

Comprehension and the Unproficient Reader

As a learner communicates through creating and reading his own language experience materials, comprehension is present. Since the language patterns, concepts, and content are familiar to even the novice reader, language experience materials should present no comprehension problems. The meaning base is the key to easing the reading task for the beginner and the remedial student. Focus on comprehension does not happen *after* some reading ability is acquired. Instead, comprehension is paramount in importance from the initial stages of reading instruction.

The very nature of the introduction to reading through language experience activities demonstrates that the reading process is for the communication of meaning. The meaning base of the language experience reading material helps the prereader and the beginning reader realize that written language represents meaning. Using meaningful written records of children's spoken thoughts provides a successful introduction to reading and writing. The greater a reader's background and experience with a given topic, the more comprehensible the material.

For children who have been diagnosed as having difficulty in comprehension, the language experience approach may be a very helpful remediation procedure. Some remedial students as well as some children in the early stages of reading instruction seem unaware that print represents meaning. For the unproficient reader, comprehension must be a high priority in instruction; language experience programs can help many students who do not read for meaning. Gradually, the remedial students should be shown that just as their personal stories represent meaning, so does the print written by others. If children regard reading only as a process of naming words, comprehension will suffer. For poor comprehenders, language experience instruction is one method for demonstrating that written language represents meaningful ideas.

Comprehension and Writing

Comprehension can be strengthened by producing language through writing. As children are writers engaged in encoding meaning with written language, they can learn much about expressing meaning effectively. Learning effective written expression can help in the acquisition of strategies for effective interpretation of the messages of others.

Supporting the contribution of writing to comprehension is the work of Applebee[5] and Brown[6] on the "sense of story." The development of sense of story is shown in the examination of children's writing and retelling of stories at different ages. Brown notes, ". . . the *extent* of a child's sense of story influences comprehension," and ". . . that the ability to 'move into' and to use the language of story is closely tied to reading achievement especially beyond the beginning stages."[7] Extensive experience with writing should contribute to children's sense of story and should enhance comprehension of features of plot structure, dialogue, character motives, and prediction of meaning. Of course, the development of the sense of story through writing is quite dependent on considerable exposure to literature through listening and reading.

As children write, they can practice and internalize schemes for organization of ideas such as outlines, main ideas and supporting details, and relation of events in a logical, ordered sequence. Through writing, students can experiment with varied styles depending on audience and purpose. Awareness from an author's viewpoint can then help in varying reading strategies according to the style, genre, and the purpose for reading. The production process of writing can facilitate the reception process of reading.

Comprehension Through Activities

The purpose of the following discussion is to show some of the powerful, yet often overlooked, potential of language experience instruction for comprehension.

Often comprehension is treated as a body of separate skills to be taught, practiced, and mastered. Comprehension is a holistic psycholinguistic process of interpreting meaning from printed language. However, to counter the argument that language experience instruction neglects the development of comprehension skills, certain comprehension tasks are identified below, and ways are cited using these tasks with language experience learning in the production of reading materials. The examples show the integration of a so-called "skill" as part of an activity that is meaning-centered. In all meaning-centered activities, the focus is on communication and interaction, not on isolated skills. A particular skill is incorporated as a natural part of a worthwhile activity and the skill itself is not the reason for the language experience learning, but instead an outcome of it. Language experience comprehension is based on involvement, relevant language, meaningful content, and language use for communication. Comprehension is central, is more than the teaching of separate skills, and focuses more on the process of comprehending than on the testing of the product of comprehension.

Prediction of meaning is significant in the comprehension process. The ease in reading the initial materials is in part due to their high predictability. Yet, such predictability may be a disadvantage if students are not shown how to use the following prediction strategies in other settings:

1. Children can be asked to predict, hypothesize, and speculate about story content when stories are to be read to them.

95

2. Students can be asked to predict content from the title or first sentence of another student's story.
3. Students can be asked to complete partial sentences and stories.
4. Modified cloze activities are used to help students with semantic and syntactic clues in sentences and passages for prediction of appropriate words.

Main ideas will be present in students' writing and can be discussed as a class in working on a group story or book. As students write titles for these group products, as well as their individual ones, main ideas will surface. As students work with composing new stories for their class and school newspapers, they can learn to develop the concept of topic sentences and lead paragraphs.

Sequence can be developed through language experience as children order the steps in a field trip, a science experiment, a recipe, or a day's schedule. Sequence can be developed as children compose personal stories, as they decide on the ordering of pages of a group book according to the plot development, as they prepare a table of contents for a group book, and as they dramatize favorite stories. A bulletin board display can be used to feature children's illustrations and text in sequential order of a story they created or retold from literature.

Summarizing can be developed in language experience programs as students retell a story they've heard for the purpose of creating an experience story or group or individual book. Accounts to be included in class and school newspapers are often summaries. Students can be shown how to provide a final summary paragraph for their writing. As students compile a reference file about books read or keep records or individual reading, they can be taught how to summarize.

Through language experiences, as noted earlier, the "sense of story" is gradually developed through exposure to hearing, reading, and writing stories. As children hear and write stories, they will incorporate in their own stories the basic features of setting, conflict, resolution, and characters. Guthrie noted that even as early as first grade, children expected stories to have a certain structure.[8]

Through language activities, children can learn to use tables of contents, indices, and glossaries as features in their writings. Even children as early as first grade can include a table of contents and a dictionary of selected words for a group book. At intermediate levels, students can organize the content by chapters and add an index. Many intermediate students will delight in including a dedication, foreword, and preface. Through *application* and *use*, the learning is probably more effective than just noting these features when encountered in other reading materials.

In language experience comprehension, the student is an active responder. Active response is encouraged not only in the production of writing but also in postreading activities featuring interpretive response through oral reactions, art, and drama. Experiencing language creatively deepens under-standing. Character traits, motives, and reactions are often best comprehended when the learner assumes the role and perspective of that character. The representation of ideas through art forms requires that the student grasp and communicate meaning personally. In these programs, active, creative involvement not only leads to the production of original material but also follows and enriches the understanding of other reading material.

Summary

Language experience instruction seeks to foster comprehension as children react to and produce written language. Even for unproficient readers, priority must be given to the meaning base for reading instruction. This method is especially helpful in showing that reading is a reconstruction of meaning from print. The writing process can strengthen comprehension since students must make their work comprehensible to others. Involvement in these activities will incorporate many facets of comprehension and relevant communication instead of isolated drill on separate skills. Comprehension is present through-out all language experience learning.

Notes

1. Kenneth S. Goodman, ed. *The Psycholinguistic Nature of the Reading Process* (Detroit: Wayne State University Press, 1968), p. 15.
2. Herbert D. Simons, "Reading Comprehension: The Need for a New Perspective," *Reading Research Quarterly* 6 (Spring 1971): 340.
3. MaryAnne Hall, Jerilyn K. Ribovich, and Christopher J. Ramig, *Reading and the Elementary School Child* (New York: Van Nostrand, 1979), p. 112.
4. Dolores Durkin, "What Classroom Observations Reveal About Reading Comprehension Instruction," *Reading Research Quarterly* 14, no. 4 (1978–79): 481–533.
5. Arthur N. Applebee, *The Child's Concept of Story* (Chicago: University of Chicago Press, 1978).
6. Garth Brown, "Development of Story in Children's Reading and Writing," *Theory into Practice* 16 (December 1977): 357–362.
7. Brown, "Development of Story in Children's Reading and Writing," p. 359.
8. John T. Guthrie, "Research Views: Story Comprehension," *The Reading Teacher* 30 (February 1977): 575.

Suggested Readings

APPLEBEE, ARTHUR N. *The Child's Concept of Story*. Chicago: University of Chicago Press, 1978. The child's "concept of story" is traced from ages two to seventeen. Six increasingly mature forms of story construction are

97

described. This description of children's language is one that can be helpful in examining comprehension and written expression.

DURKIN, DOLORES. "What Classroom Observations Reveal about Reading Comprehension Instruction," *Reading Research Quarterly* 14 (No. 4, 1978–79): 481–533. This study reveals that comprehension instruction in the classroom is almost nonexistent. Teachers spent more time assessing than instructing.

HALL, MARYANNE; RIBOVICH, JERILYN K.; and RAMIG, CHRISTOPHER J. *Reading and the Elementary School Child.* New York: Van Nostrand, 1979. This textbook for teachers includes discussion of the teaching of comprehension. Chapters 4, 5, and 6 feature comprehension for beginners, primary graders, and intermediate levels.

PEARSON, P. DAVID, and JOHNSON, DALE D. *Teaching Reading Comprehension.* New York: Holt, Rinehart & Winston, 1978. The active role of the reader is stressed throughout the discussion of comprehension from schema theory and a psycholinguistic base.

SMITH, FRANK. *Comprehension and Learning.* New York: Holt, Rinehart & Winston, 1975. Smith's discussion of comprehension is a psycholinguistic analysis. His description of the "theory of the world in the head" stresses the significance of a learner's prior knowledge for "making sense" in reading as in all learning.

SMITH, RICHARD J., and BARRETT, THOMAS. *Teaching Reading in the Middle Grades.* Reading, Mass.: Addison-Wesley, 1979. Thoughtful activities for promoting reading comprehension are included, and a number of the activities with literature could be extended to language experience ones. Also included here is Barrett's Taxonomy of Reading Comprehension.

STAUFFER, RUSSELL G. *Directing the Reading Thinking Process.* New York: Harper and Row, 1975. Stauffer's discussion of pupil purpose-setting to encourage predicting, hypothesizing, and speculating and thus thinking is of great significance in the effective teaching of reading.

8

Prereading in the Language Experience Approach

Prereading, the stage of reading development that precedes the formal introduction to reading, is the base upon which future success and attitudes toward reading are built. Readiness for reading comes from a base of past experience, maturation, and training. A successful experience from the first stages should be the goal for every beginning reader. No sharp dividing line between prereading and beginning reading should exist, but instead there should be a gradual transition from one level of reading development to the next.

Readiness for reading is a multidimensional composite of a number of linguistic, cognitive, physiological, perceptual, social-emotional, and experiential factors. However, a broad view of readiness should not obscure the need for carefully focused instruction on specific skills needed for successful beginning reading. With language experience programs, the overall readiness is, of course, important. The intent here is to identify selected concerns and to explain language experience instruction directed toward development of these prereading areas.

Language and experience are two important cornerstones on which readiness for reading is built. A language experience program can provide the foundation for a successful start in learning to read and can relate reading to the child's existing level of language development. One basic understanding that children should develop as a base for successful beginning reading is that written language is a code for meaning along with the concept that reading is for the purpose of communication.[1] Meaningful instruction in the visual discrimination, visual memory, auditory discrimination, letter names, left-to-right progression across a line of print, and language concepts can be provided with pupil-composed materials in a language experience framework. Improving oral language facility in speaking and listening and developing an interest in reading are also concerns in the prereading period.

The language experience approach provides a natural transition from prereading to beginning reading as children are exposed to their oral language encoded in written form with personal and group experience stories. The language experience approach clearly demonstrates the relationship between spoken and written language and helps children recognize that print conveys meaning. When children first use experience stories, they may be unable to recognize any words. Gradually, however, they do learn to identify words, thus acquiring a reading vocabulary and moving into the beginning reading stage.

The language experience approach uses functional situations with oral and written language drawn from personal experiences to develop prereading skills. This approach to prereading is not dependent upon commercial materials, although a teacher may wish to combine language experience materials with selected commercial materials. This chapter is not intended to present a complete program of instruction in prereading; rather, its intent is to describe how the language experience approach can be implemented to teach the important understandings of the prereading period. While language experience is often thought of as beginning reading instead of a prereading program, there are a number of prereading applications for language experience learning.

A theme of this chapter might be "teach prereading skills in a reading situation." Print should be used in prereading to prepare children to deal with print in beginning reading. Certain readiness concepts can best be developed with written language. Many commercial readiness materials contain no or very little print. By using a reading situation to teach prereading skills children can receive useful instruction that is applicable to the demands of beginning reading. It is ironic that some prereading programs deprive children of the very training needed for success in beginning reading. Nonprint situations cannot provide the development needed in visual discrimination and left-to-right orientation, which should be shown with printed words. For slow starters, especially, the prereading period may be extremely wasteful since these children may be deprived of the very experiences that would develop readiness for reading. Exposure to print is of prime importance in the development of readiness for reading. Children need experience with meaningful written language to develop the understanding that print represents meaning. Another reason for recommending exposure to written language in the prereading program is that such exposure may lead to interest in learning to write, which in turn may serve as a key to motivating interest in reading.[2,3]

There are many avenues to reading. For example, leading children to reading by recording their speech is a very natural way of leading children into reading. Using children's art work to initiate oral expression of ideas to be recorded with print is another natural transition from prereading to beginning reading.

With exposure to relevant experience materials, beginners should have an introduction to reading that presents written language in purposeful situations. However, experience materials often are used in such a general way that students may not get the specific training in visual discrimination, left-to-right sequence, visual memory, and language concepts essential for success in beginning reading. Attention must be focused on the appropriate cues in the print, even though the natural, relevant, and functional setting of language experience reading should not be sacrificed for skill instruction. Both the meaningful communication setting and focused skill instruction can be offered in a thorough language experience program. In the following discussion of specific content, use of language experience materials focusing on prereading in a reading situation is recommended.

Print Represents Meaning

Even before learning to read, children should grasp that print represents meaning and that the purpose of reading is communication. Children see print on signs, billboards, cereal boxes, toothpaste, soap, Coke bottles, and television. Children who have been read to and observed parents reading also have encountered invaluable exposure to print. Prereading program activities with print should feature relevant content that children understand. Smith observes that although young children have noticed the print around them and know that print is meaningful, often the beginning teaching erases this original insight.[4] Unfortunately, some instruction with print starts with isolated letters and stresses "basic" words without meaningful content with the natural language of sentence and stories.

Experience charts and other child-authored stories and materials are essential in prereading as well as in beginning reading. With prereaders, the material will be read to them instead of by them independently, but it is important to have "real" reading to convey that the written language is a representation of meaning.

Preparation for reading occurs through encounters with real print and real communication. Immersion in the language experience activities is an excellent natural introduction to print. Stress on isolated nonlanguage based readiness lessons does not result in children's internalization of reading as communication and of print as a representation of meaning.

101

Visual Discrimination and Visual Memory

Prereading teaching should emphasize visual discrimination and visual memory. Visual discrimination of likenesses and differences in letters and words is required in learning to read. Visual memory requires not only the ability to recognize likenesses and differences in printed language but also to remember a visual image of a form. To attach a name to a printed symbol is essential to learning to read, and readers must be able to retain associations or labels for printed stimuli.

Discrimination activities with letters and words have been found to be more valuable than activities with nonword forms[5]. Distinguishing similarities and differences between letters and between words relates directly to the perceptual tasks involved in reading, whereas discriminating between pictures in a row or discriminating between geometric forms is not the same visual task as that required in reading.

Smith[6] and Samuels[7] have commented that the memory of word and letter forms is related to learning distinctive features of the forms. Research confirms that when the distinctive features of letters are pointed out to prereaders, better performance in learning letter names and better discrimination have resulted than when training has not included attention to distinctive features.

Visual discrimination is explored in this activity.

Samuels[8] has presented a probing examination of research related to factors involved in success and failure in beginning reading. His examination of the research indicates that both simultaneous (matching with example shown) and successive (discrimination with example removed) training in visual discrimination should be given to facilitate learning distinctive features and to develop classification systems for memory or printed forms.

The pupil-composed materials of the language experience approach offer many opportunities for teaching both simultaneous and successive visual discrimination in a reading situation. For example, with the first experience stories in kindergarten and grade one, the teacher can have children match letter, word, phrase, and sentence cards to letters, words, phrases, and sentences on the charts. (See chapter 3.) This type of activity relates visual discrimination to a reading situation as children are working with meaningful content. Careful attention to the placing of the cards being matched under the appropriate corresponding material can assist in developing skill in simultaneous discrimination. While simultaneous discrimination is common, successive discrimination is often overlooked. This type also can occur in language experience situations if after showing a particular letter, phrase, or word or sentence card, the card is removed so that children must select the appropriate response from memory. This training of memory for word forms should aid in learning reading vocabulary.

In an activity such as writing daily plans with the class, the teacher can call the pupils' attention to the repetition of certain words. For example, plans such as the following could be written:

> We will read.
> We will write a story.
> We will play outside.
> We will have music.

The teacher can ask, "What do you notice about the first word in each line?" "What do you notice about the second word?" Word, phrase, and sentence cards can be used for matching.

In the above examples, the words have meaning for the prereaders even though they are not able to identify the words in other contexts. In the examples cited the teacher said the word, phrase, or sentence for the children to match. Pupils at this level do not have to read words to respond to the task of matching visually. However, the teacher should use the word *read* in the explanations so that the children will realize that reading involves recognizing what the print represents.

Pupils' names provide another source for visual discrimination activities. A class roll chart with all the children's names can be used for matching activities. Each pupil can have an individual card with his name, and these cards can be matched to the names on the roll chart. Names with similar forms and letters can be grouped together to encourage fine discrimination. For example, names as similar as *Larry* and *Harry, Tommy* and *Timmy,* and *Pat, Patricia,* and *Patrick* should be grouped together.

103

Using pupils' names for other visual discrimination acitivies is also recommended. For example, a chart with horizontal rows of names can be made, and children can be directed to find all the names like the first one. The interest and motivation is usually high when pupil names are used. Names of objects in the room also can be used for teaching children to notice the first word in a line and then to identify all the other words in the line that are identical to the first one.

LETTER NAMES

In many readiness programs, letter names are taught. The significance of learning letter names prior to beginning reading may have been overstressed in recent years because of emphasis on the research findings that knowledge of letter names correlates more highly with reading achievement at the end of grade one than other factors.[9] The researchers caution that correlation is not the same as cause and effect. Some research has found that direct instruction in letter names does not improve achievement in beginning reading.[10,11] While prereading teaching should include letter name knowledge as part of the program, false assumptions about the value of this instruction should be avoided.

One explanation of why a correlation exists between letter name knowledge and first grade reading achievement might be that the letter name variable is easy to identify and to test. Children who come to school knowing letter names often bring a wide variety of information and the letter knowledge is just one part of the broad background they bring with them. Also, children who easily learn to attach a name to an abstract symbol may succeed more in reading than those who have difficulty associating letter names and symbols. Knowing letter names is more than correctly saying the alphabet. It is possible for a child to recite the alphabet and not know the name of a letter when shown its printed form. Children should understand that words are made up of letters and should be able to associate letter forms with letter names. Instruction in letter names is part of the "exposure" philosophy of the language experience learning in the prereading period.

Letter names can be taught in functional situations since children are constantly being exposed to letters in charts, chalkboard writing, their names, and personal experience stories. The name and experience charts suggested for visual discrimination can also be used for letter matching activities. Each child should have an individual set of all uppercase and lowercase letters to be used in the matching activities. The teacher can point to a name on the chart and ask the children to hold up the letter that they see at the beginning of that name. The name of the letter is stated by the teacher or children. In each case the name of the child should be read by the teacher so that the children realize the letter forms are used as parts of meaningful words.

The children can use their individual sets of letter cards for practice in learning letter names. Every child can respond if each has his own set of cards. For example, the teacher can say when pointing to a word on an experience chart or on the chalkboard, "This word begins with a capital *M*. Can all of you hold up your cards with capital *M*? Now you can find a little *m*?" The teacher should praise the correct responses and note those children needing additional practice.

ABC books of children's literature can be read to children to promote interest in letters. A number of the attractively illustrated and imaginatively written ABC books, such as *Bruno Munari's ABC,* by Bruno Munari,[12] *ABC of Cars and Trucks,* by Anne Alexander,[13] or Jan Garten's *An Alphabet Tale,*[14] should be available in the classroom library corner for pupils to examine independently. Pupils can develop their own ABC books with illustrations for each of the letters. In developing these books, letter sounds should not be stressed since confusion can result at this stage if children are confronted with the multiple associations in the sound-letter relationships of the language. In making class and indivdual ABC books the emphasis is on the names and forms of letters.

Other activities can contribute to learning letter names. Learning to write directs children's attention to the names and forms of letters. As letters are used in visual discrimination training, the teacher may say, "Can you find all the *1's* in this line?" Boxes of letters may be available on the reading table, and children can be encouraged to build words to match the words in group and personal experience stories. Children can work in pairs in naming letters.

Auditory Discrimination

Learning to discriminate likenesses and differences in the sounds of spoken words has long been part of readiness programs. Prereading instruction in auditory discrimination provides a base for later instruction in phonics. While authorities differ on the importance of auditory discrimination for learning to read, a prereading program will ordinarily include auditory discrimination and memory training as part of the total program.

As was true with letter name instruction, the significance of auditory discrimination in success in reading is debatable. Durrell believes that attention to distinguishing the separate sounds of spoken words is the most neglected subskill in readiness training.[15] Samuels comments, "Few areas in psychology present a more perplexing picture with conflicting viewpoints than the area of auditory discrimination."[16] Samuels comments further,

The literature on auditory discrimination and reading leads one to conclude that in the absence of frank sensory impairment reading difficulty is probably not strongly associated with lack of auditory discrimination. Although auditory discrimination does not seem to be an important problem for the student learning to read, memory for letter names, sounds, or words appears to be of greater importance.[17]

Children at the beginning of grade one usually bring considerable auditory discrimination of language with them. They have learned the phonemes of their language since at the time of school entrance in first grade they can produce the phonemes of their language as evidenced by their speech. Probably what teachers mean when they say that children need training in auditory discrimination is that children need to learn the meaning of terms such as *sound, beginning sound, ending sound, rhyme,* and where they need to focus their attention for learning sound-symbol correspondences.

Some children do poorly on auditory discrimination tests partly because

1. lack of comprehension of the directions,
2. words in isolation and may not pronounced by the examiner as they are in the child's speech, and
3. lack of familiarity with the task required rather than lack of the ability to discriminate.

In initial reading instruction attention is given to the *association* of a sound with the printed letter symbol. Prior to that type of instruction, the ability to discriminate similarities and differences in sounds in spoken words is featured.

Activities

Numerous opportunities for auditory discrimination grow out of language experience activities. As group experience charts are written with pupils, attention can be directed to words on a chart that begin with the same sound. For example, with the chart on p. 37 the teacher might say, "Listen as I say these words: *carrots, cabbage; go, get.* Listen for the first sound in them."

The name chart described on p. 103 can also be used for auditory discrimination as the teacher can ask pupils to listen for similarities in the beginning sounds of several names such as *Jack, Johnny, Joyce.* Groups of three names, two of which have the same beginning sound and one with a different beginning sound, can be used as children are asked to indicate which two names begin alike.

In personal experience stories, teachers can point out to a child that two or more words begin with the same sound and have him say the words to hear the sound. Work on rhyming words should also be included when examples of these words appear in the group and individual experience stories.

Some children who may seem confused about auditory discrimination activities with words may need some experiences to develop the concept of "sound" and "alike and different." For children who seem unable to distinguish between letter sounds in spoken words, more gross auditory discrimination may be advisable. To develop an awareness of sounds in the environment before progressing to letter sounds, children's literature books such as *The Listening Walk*, by Paul Showers[18] and the series of "Noisy Books," by Margaret Wise Brown,[19] can be very helpful.

Left-to-Right Direction

Following a line of print from left-to-right is a requirement of the reading act, and the correct orientation to the printed page must be established in the prereading period. Developing the habit of observing printed words and sentences from left-to-right should be part of the experience with written language in prereading. Language experience materials can be used to demonstrate left-to-right sequence in reading situations. In other words, left-to-right is taught not by observing rows of pictures but with printed letters and words, thereby relating the training to the reading task. The activities for teaching left-to-right progression encourages the natural relationship of this skill to the actual reading situation.

As the teacher writes and reads plans, she can show left-to-right direction by telling pupils that in writing one always starts at the left side and goes to the right. As the teacher reads, she should move her hand under the words. In the reading of all group experience stories, the direction can be demonstrated by the teacher's hand movement or a pointer. As pupils match cards to a chart, the teacher can show left-to-right direction. In working with personal experience stories, the teacher can show individual pupils how print is read from left-to-right. As pupils underline words on the board, on a chart, or in a personal experience story, the teacher again can encourage left-to-right progression. As pupils learn to do manuscript writing, they should be taught direction also. Of course, game-type activities with left and right directions such as "Simon Says" and "Looby Loo" can be used.

Oral Language

Increasing oral language facility is another concern in the prereading program since to comprehend and express ideas through oral language contributes to meaningful reading. Oral language performance and competence is the base on which performance and competence in written language is built. Both receptive language use through listening and productive language use through speaking are important. There must be content worth listening to and talking about. However, starting with pupil backgrounds, the teacher must not limit the pupils' exposure to only that language and those experiences they presently possess. It is the teacher's obligation to extend the experience background and language competence and performance. In this approach with the integration of speaking, listening, reading, and writing, oral language experiences receive considerable attention.

Children must be encouraged to talk in situations where they may feel free to express themselves regardless of their level of language development and speech patterns; talk when stimuli for conversation and discussion are ample and ever-changing; talk where pupil talk is more important than teacher talk; talk in situations where they are exposed to new experiences, new vocabulary, and new thoughts through tapes, stories, trips, films, pictures, drama, and conversations; and talk in an environment where their talk is the basis for other language experiences as they compose group and personal experience stories and class and individual books as they listen to the ideas of others and state their own, and as they read their ideas.

Language Concepts

Developing children's concepts of language and awareness of features of written language should be included in prereading and beginning reading instruction. It is well known that most children who enter kindergarten and first grade bring with them considerable language mastery. While this competence is far from complete, the child's level of linguistic development does include using the basic sentence patterns of the native language, knowing the meaning of thousands of words, and communicating both as a language receiver and language producer. While the linguistic performance and competence are extensive, children are often confused by the terminology used in beginning reading. Evans, Taylor, and Blum report that linguistic awareness reflected by tasks that stress the interrelatedness of oral and written language is related to reading achievement for first grade children.[20] Children need to learn the language of instruction so that the terms *word, letter, sentence,* and *sound* are not confusing ones. The connection between spoken and written language is also part of developing children's awareness of written language. This awareness requires exposure to print in prereading.

Language experience materials are particularly valuable in developing children's metalinguistic awareness. In the matching activities suggested for visual discrimination, the concepts of word, phrase, letter, and sentence can be demonstrated functionally. The orientation to written language offered with experience stories can provide a base for developing the concepts of language often lacking in the prereading and beginning reading stages.

Interest in Reading

Before formal instruction in reading is begun, children want to read. Children who have been read to at home, nursery school, and kindergarten have experienced pleasurable contacts with books. For those children who have not had such contacts, providing opportunities to hear stories and examine the attractive picture-story books is even more important. The most effective means for developing an interest in reading is through exposure to interesting children's literature materials. Realizing that meaning comes from the printed page and that reading is an enjoyable experience are understandings conveyed through hearing stories read aloud. Every classroom should contain an attractive library corner, and every classroom should feature a daily period of story reading by the teacher.

The personal pride that results from pupil authorship also has a favorable effect on pupil interest. The group and individual experience stories written with children in the prereading and beginning reading stages should foster enthusiasm for reading since the content is of high interest to pupils. If the introduction to reading occurs in a functional situation, interest should be inherent in that situation. Success with the pupil-composed materials should also have a favorable effect on attitude and interest.

Summary

One of the most significant contributions of language experience instruction to the prereading stages is the development of the general understanding that print represents meaning. Prereading instruction in visual discrimination and memory, letter names, auditory discrimination, left-to-right progression, language development, language concepts, and interest in reading can be approached from a language experience framework. Particular emphasis is placed on encouraging oral language development since this is the base from which other language experiences grow. Children's oral language forms the basis of pupil-produced materials, which can be used for instruction in prereading.

In the language experience approach, the prereading stage blends gradually into the beginning reading stage through the use of group experience charts and personal stories. The approach to prereading illustrates the relationship between spoken and written language. Prereading training develops understandings needed for beginning reading in a reading situation with functional, pupil-developed materials rather than with artificial materials remote from children's experiences. Prereading and beginning reading are introduced in a realistic reading situation that fosters success and healthy attitudes toward self and toward learning.

Notes

1. Eleanor Gibson and Harry Levin, *The Psychology of Reading* (Cambridge, Mass.: MIT Press, 1975), p. 323.
2. Dolores Durkin, "A Six Year Study of Children Who Learned to Read in School at the Age of Four," *Reading Research Quarterly* 10, no. 1 (1974–1975):11.
3. Marie Clay, *What Did I Write?* (Auckland, New Zealand: Heinemann Educational Books Limited, 1975).
4. Frank Smith, "Making Sense of Reading and Reading Instruction," *Harvard Educational Review* 47 (August 1977):386–395.
5. Thomas A. Barrett, "The Relationship between Measures of Prereading Visual Discrimination and First Grade Reading Achievement: A Review of the Literature," *Reading Research Quarterly* 1 (Fall 1965):51.
6. Frank Smith, *Understanding Reading* (New York: Holt, Rinehart & Winston, 1971): pp. 105–121.
7. S. Jay Samuels, "Success and Failure in Learning to Read: A Critique of the Research," *Reading Research Quarterly* 8 (Winter 1973):213.
8. Samuels, "Success and Failure. . . ."
9. Guy L. Bond and Robert Dykstra. "The Cooperative Research Program in First Grade Reading Programs," *Reading Research Quarterly* 2 (Summer 1967):116.
10. D. D. Ohnmacht, "The Effects of Letter Knowledge on Achievement in Reading in First Grade," Paper presented at American Educational Research Association, Los Angeles, California, February 1969.
11. S. Jay Samuels, "The Effect of Letter Name Knowledge on Learning to Read," *American Educational Research Journal* 9 (Winter 1972):65–74.
12. Bruno Munari, *Bruno Munari's ABC* (New York: The World Publishing Company, 1960).
13. Anne Alexander, *ABC of Cars and Trucks* (New York: Doubleday & Company, 1956).
14. Jan Garten, *An Alphabet Tale* (New York: Random House, 1964).
15. Donald D. Durrell, "Learning Factors in Beginning Reading," in *Teaching Young Children to Read,* ed. Warren G. Cutts (Washington, D.C.: U.S. Office of Education, 1964), p. 72.
16. Samuels, "Success and Failure," p. 226.
17. Samuels, pp. 232–33.
18. Paul Showers, *The Listening Walk* (New York: Crowell Collier & Macmillan, 1961).
19. For example, see Margaret Wise Brown, *The City Noisy Book* (New York: Harper & Row, 1939).
20. Martha Evans, Nancy Taylor, and Irene Blum, "Children's Written Language Awareness and Its Relation to Reading Acquisition," *Journal of Reading Behavior* 11 (Spring 1979): 7–19.

Suggested Readings

DURKIN, DOLORES. *Teaching Young Children to Read.* Boston: Allyn and Bacon, 1976. Durkin presents a thorough consideration of the topic of readiness and gives detailed descriptions for instruction in prereading and beginning reading.

EVANS, MARTHA; TAYLOR, NANCY; and BLUM, IRENE. "Children's Written Language Awareness and Its Relation to Reading Acquisition," *Journal of Reading Behavior* 11 (Spring 1979): 7–19. This report of the development and use of an instrument composed of language awareness tasks for readiness assessment shows that aspects of written language awareness can be identified and measured systematically.

HALL, MARYANNE; RIBOVICH, JERILYN K.; and RAMIG, CHRISTOPHER J. *Reading and the Elementary School Child.* New York: Van Nostrand, 1979. Chapter 3 discusses prereading—definitions, factors influencing readiness, and instructional program content and procedures.

LEE, DORRIS M., and ALLEN, R. VAN. *Learning to Read through Experience.* New York: Appleton-Century-Crofts, 1963. This basic source on the language experience approach gives many examples of the transition from prereading to initial reading instruction. The philosophy of the language experience approach as a natural introduction to reading is a basic theme of this book.

OLLILA, LLOYD O., ed. *The Kindergarten Child and Reading.* Newark, Del.: International Reading Association, 1977. This pamphlet discusses issues in prereading including the age of learning to read and the nature of prereading and beginning reading for kindergarten children.

SAMUELS, S. JAY. "Success and Failure in Learning to Read: A Critique of the Research," *Reading Research Quarterly* 8 (Winter 1973): 200–39. This source is recommended for a thoughtful analysis of research related to reading in the beginning stages.

SMITH, FRANK. "Making Sense of Reading and Reading Instruction," *Harvard Educational Review* 47 (August 1977): 386–395. Smith discusses two insights he believes are essential for beginning reading. One is that print is meaningful and the other is that spoken and written language are different.

9
Word Analysis Strategies in the Language Experience Approach

The theory and techniques of the preceding chapters have been concerned with teaching children to read effectively. Because the language experience approach is so concerned with reading as communication through language symbols, the place of word analysis instruction may be unclear for several reasons. First, since in this approach reading is viewed as a *process* rather than as a collection of skills, skills do not determine the instructional content. Second, since the approach is built from pupils' oral language, the dimension of strategies for independent word identification may not be clearly recognized. Third, since this is an integrated approach with the language skills taught through pupil composition and experiences with spoken and written language, a teacher may not be clear about the types and amounts of direct word analysis teaching needed. Fourth, the language experience approach is not one with a clear, systematic sequence of learning according to a predetermined guide.

The purpose of this chapter is to identify selected word analysis content and to suggest means of incorporating that content in the language experience framework. In word analysis instruction, as in other language experience learning, attention must be on language as communication—not on small portions of that language which are devoid of meaning without context.

Word analysis has been accorded immense attention in the teaching of reading. In fact, in some reading programs the emphasis on phonics and other word analysis content seems disproportionate when considered in connection with attention to meaningful reading. It's important to remember that the bulk of the time in language experience programs is with meaningful whole language and not on the study of isolated parts of language. Focus on phoneme-grapheme correspondences and on rules may put too much stress on the word and letter units of language instead of on larger units of meaning. Teaching children to recognize and respond to printed language is broader than the teaching of what is traditionally referred to as word analysis. Perhaps the use of the term *language recognition* or *processing* might be more appropriate than the terms *word attack, word analysis,* or *word recognition.* Effective teaching strategies in language experience reading rest upon having children develop language processing strategies to deal with graphophonic, semantic, and syntactic language information. In fact, much of the material in previous chapters is more related to language processing than the material included here with the word analysis label.

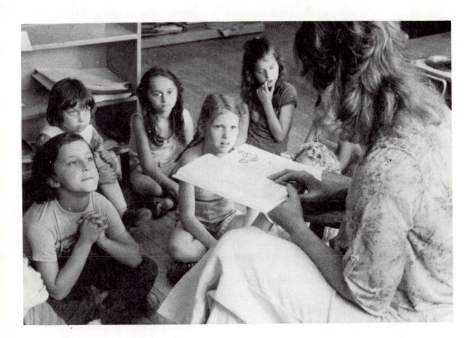

Children enjoy hearing literature read aloud.

Any reading program must teach children methods of analyzing unfamiliar words quickly and independently. Each teacher should know about the content of word analysis, provide both direct and incidental instruction, and evaluate children's learning in this area. In order to strengthen the

113

reading program while following this approach, some authorities recommend that the teacher follow a systematic program in word analysis in addition to the other language experience activities.

Flexible grouping is recommended since groups will be formed according to need for a common learning and will either be disbanded or modified in composition as needs change. Teachers can follow checklists for phonics and structural analysis, keep records for each child in order to note mastery, and indicate the content that needs to be learned. Many teachers keep a notebook or file box of informal observations about each child's reading performance.

The language experience approach does offer an excellent means for introducing and reinforcing word analysis in functional situations. This method can teach strategies as needed by pupils in their independent reading and writing. Pupils' language in the group and individual stories and in word banks will provide examples for word analysis. In the investigation of research on this approach, Hall notes the concern that word analysis instruction may be slighted,[1] but research by Baxley and Dzama shows that the vocabulary used by children and reflected in the word banks furnishes children with ample examples for studying the common word analysis generalizations.[2,3]

The word analysis content discussed here is classified by phonics, structural or morphemic analysis, and meaning cues, which include context, semantic, and syntactic cues. Dictionary use is also featured.

Phonics

Phonics instruction is concerned with the teaching of the association of phonemes (units of sound) with graphemes (units of written language). The purpose of teaching phonics is to provide readers with a tool for identification of unknown words. However, phonics alone is not an adequate word analysis system.

In working with phonics in the language experience approach, an analytic approach studying speech sounds in whole words is preferred rather than studying single sounds in isolation. In an analytic approach, known words are used in developing an understanding of the phoneme-grapheme (sound-letter) relationships of the language.

In teaching the association of a sound with its printed counterpart, the teacher must provide auditory and visual experience with the sound and letter form and must demonstrate the application of the phoneme-grapheme relationship to attack an unfamiliar word in context. Since phonics instruction aims to give children a tool for attacking unfamiliar words, the application step must be stressed. For example, in working with the initial sound of *m,* the teacher may group several children together and ask them to find all of the words in their word banks that begin with *m*. The instruction should include hearing the sound of *m* as the words are said aloud. Then, several words familiar to all the pupils should be listed so that children can see the visual form of *m* in whole word forms. Then some sentences can be written with a new word beginning with *m* in each sentence. The children can attack these words by using the phonic and context clues. Examples might be, "When it is cold, you wear *mittens,*" or "The *milk* is white." The children can be told that they know all the words except the one beginning with *m* and are told to think of a word that would make sense in each sentence. Words that are already known by children can be used to illustrate the consonant substitution technique for attacking new words. The teacher might say, "You know the word *ten.* What word do you have if the *t* is changed to an *m?*" Additional examples such as *bat* to *mat, six* to *mix* could be used.

A similar procedure can be followed in teaching the sound-letter relationships of the other consonants, the consonant blends or clusters, the consonant digraphs, and the vowels. A sample lesson plan showing the steps mentioned above is reproduced below.[4] Note the importance of context in the application step.

LESSON PLAN: A PHONEME-GRAPHEME CORRESPONDENCE LESSON (BEGINNING READING)

Previous Learnings Assumed

It is assumed that children have learned the phoneme-grapheme correspon-dences for the consonants *r, m,* and *b.* No value judgment is implied in the order: the lesson is merely structured in such a manner as to require the learnings of these three phoneme-grapheme correspondences.

It is also assumed that children have three or four words beginning with *w* in their reading vocabulary which act as stimulus words, and that all words except the context sentences in the application step are in their reading vocabularies.

Objectives

General Objective The general objective of this lesson is to develop independence in word analysis.

Specific Objectives As a result of this lesson, children should be able to
- Recognize the sound of *w* in spoken words by responding with the appropriate *yes* or *no* card.
- Attack new words in reading by applying context clues and the initial consonant sound represented by *w.*
- Attack new words in reading by using consonant substitution.

115

Materials

- Magazine pictures to illustrate sentences in application step.
- Every-pupil response cards for *w, r, m, b, yes,* and *no.*

Procedures

Auditory Experience Several activities can provide auditory experience with the sound of *w* in spoken words.

- The teacher may say, "Listen to the word *wagon* . . . *wagon.* . . . Now I am going to say some words. Listen to see if they begin like *wagon.* I will say *wagon* and then another word. If the words begin alike, hold up your *yes* card. If they do not sound alike at the beginning, hold up your *no* card. Ready?"

  The word pairs might include *wagon/want, wagon/boy, wagon/rabbit wagon/wonderful, wagon/watch, wagon/month* (Note: the phonemes are not presented in isolation. Instead, whole words are used as children are asked to listen for the similarity at the beginning of words.)

- Or the teacher might comment "You have already learned the sounds you hear when *r, m,* and *b* are the first letters in a word. Remember that *w* is the letter at the beginning of *wagon.* This time hold up the card that shows the first letter in the words I say, Ready?" The teacher then pronounces a list of words, for example: *monkey, watch, witch, rose, run, book, mark, with, big.*

- To provide practice with oral context, the following type of activity could be used. The teacher asks, "Can you think of a word begining like *wagon* which could be used in these sentences?"

  You can _____ a sweater.
  There are pictures on the _____.

Visual Presentation Visual presentation of the phoneme-grapheme relationship might be accomplished in the following way. The teacher writes *we, will,* and *want* on the chalkboard and comments, "Here are some words you know how to read. What is the first letter you see in these words?"

After the children have identified *w,* the teacher asks, "Show me your letter card for *w* (letter name). (Note: where we have used a single letter we mean for the teacher to name the letter but not to try to say the phoneme represented by the letter.) Does *we* sound like *wagon* at the beginning? . . . What about *want* and *wagon*? . . . What about *will* and *wagon*?"

Association Association of the phoneme with the grapheme that represents it can be accomplished, again referring to the list of words, by the teacher asking, "How are the words in this list alike? . . . That's right, they all begin with *w* (letter name). They look alike, and they sound alike at the beginning. You know that the letter *w* stands for the sound you hear at the beginning of these words."

Application Using magazine pictures that correspond to sentences containing a new word beginning with *w*, the teacher may say, "Now, let's see if you can figure out some new words that begin with *w*. You know all the words except the ones beginning with *w*. Read the sentence I write for each picture, and think of a word that makes sense in the sentence."

Examples might include

> The girl is looking out the *window*.
> The street is *wide*.
> The boy has a glass of *water*.
> The family likes to *watch* TV.

It should be noted that the purpose is not for all children to commit these words to their reading vocabularies but to provide practice in using both context and the phoneme-grapheme correspondence clues to attack unfamiliar words.

Further Practice For additional practice in consonant substitution with the letter *w,* the teacher might write or display a chart containing the following list of words:

get	ball	make	ride	tent	pin
_et	_all	_ake	_ide	_ent	_in

She would also say to the children. "Here are some words you know. If the first letter of the first word is changed to *w* you have a different word." The teacher will write *w* as the first letter of the word in all the examples and will ask the children to read all the resulting words.

In future reading situations children should be asked to look for words that begin with *w*. In this way they can find words (and even pictures) to add to a *w* chart in the classroom.

Structural Analysis

Structural or morphemic analysis involves studying unfamiliar words by analyzing word parts or morphemic units. A morpheme is the smallest unit of meaning in the language. Children are taught to look for the parts of com-

117

pound words, roots, prefixes, suffixes, contractions, and known syllables. The last part of the word analysis checklist (chart 1) lists the major categories of structural analysis. Flexible grouping of pupils for direct teaching is recommended while working with the checklist content.

Structural analysis is taught through examples from the personal and group experience stories and the word banks. Structural analysis of prefixes and suffixes should be illustrated in sentence context. In working with prefixes and suffixes, the teacher must emphasize meaning, not just form or pronunciation. It is more valuable for a child to use meaningful sentences to decide whether *wish, wishes, wished,* or *wishing* is appropriate than merely to drill or write the word *wish* with endings, since it is only in a sentence context that a child will know which form is appropriate.

Botel describes a discovery procedure for developing the understanding of generalizations. Children are given auditory and visual examples with a particular pattern. They are then directed to observe the pattern through careful teacher questioning, collect words that follow the pattern, and formulate the appropriate generalization for the pattern.[5] For example, if children were working with the structural change generalization in which the final consonant is doubled in a word having a consonant-vowel-consonant (*hop*) pattern before adding an ending, the discovery procedure would work as follows: The teacher could write several pairs of sentences such as, "Jack will bat next, "He has a good batting average," or "The car will stop at the light, "The car has stopped." She could then ask, "Can you find the root word in *batting*?" "Does the ending begin with a vowel or a consonant?" "What is added to the root word before adding the ending?" "Look at the last three letters of the root words." Children should note the consonant-vowel-consonant pattern of the root words. They can be asked to find words in their reading which fit this pattern. In the inductive learning of this procedure, the children state the generalization after specific examples are studied.

The preceding procedure can be used in a reading regardless of the instructional approach. However, in the language experience method, the distinctive characteristic is the selection of words from the children's writing. The procedure can also be applied to the examples listed in chart 1 for vowel generalizations, syllabication generalizations, and structural analysis.

Meaning Cues

Meaning cues for word analysis are context, semantic, syntactic, and expectancy cues. These cues operate together in the reading process, and meaningful content and the surrounding context do influence word analysis, since a reader uses prediction, prior knowledge, and expectancy as he reads. Semantic cues are those cues related to the meaning and concepts for the vocabulary in a selection, while syntactic cues are those clues to meaning signalled by the grammatical relationships of elements in a sentence. Children using language experience materials should develop "sentence sense," which should result in both expecting and supplying meaning while they read.

The following examples of meaning cues are from Hall, Ribovich, and Ramig.[6]

1. Suppose the only new word is *picnic*.

    It was a nice summer day so we decided to go on a *picnic*. We packed some food and drove to the park and ate outside.

    The child who has the conceptual and experience background for picnic can deal with the new printed word *picnic* without difficulty. Notice, too, that the context clue for the meaning of *picnic* comes in the sentence after the one in which the word is first used. If oral reading is required before silent reading, children will be unable to use the context clues effectively.

2. Suppose the only new word is *pilot*.

    Nancy was going on a trip in an airplane. She thought that it would be wonderful to be a *pilot* and fly airplanes.

    Again, the expectancy clues triggered by the information background related to airplanes and a concept of *pilot* would cue the reader for the appropriate word.

3. Suppose the only new word is *secret*.

    David would not tell. He would keep the *secret*.

    The meaning cue here is obvious from the context of these two short sentences. In a story with this example, there would probably be additional prior cues from the total story context.

4. Suppose the only new word for the reader is *silo*.

    The farmer stored his grain in the *silo*.

    The child who has heard the word *silo* used before in conversational settings, or who has some knowledge about farms either from firsthand experience or from books or TV, will use expectancy cues to supply an appropriate word. The beginner without any experience with farms or the concept of *silo* will find this particular word more difficult than the child who has the background to use expectancy cues in this instance.

    A beginner will also learn to use the contextual cue in conjunction with the initial letter cue to narrow the possibilities for the proper word choice. Some children might use the context in the above example to suggest *barn,* but then the teacher might say, "Yes *barn* will make sense, but this word begins like *Sam* and *summer.* Is there another word that tells where grain or crops might be stored?" If children cannot answer this question, then the need is to develop the concept of *silo* instead of drilling on sound-letter correspondences. If a word is outside the reader's realm of

119

experience and not in his listening or speaking vocabulary, then phonics is of no value at all.

The need for working with words in context is illustrated by the following examples. In these examples with homographs the syntactic and semantic clues operate together to signal meaning. The context is necessary to know which pronunciation is appropriate.

Tony likes to *read*.

Lions *live* in the jungle.

Jenny liked her birthday *present*.

He *read* three books last week.

Live animals need food and water.

The principal will *present* the award.

An activity that can be used to show the use of combined context and phonic cues is a modified cloze procedure, in which the first letter or first two letters of words are given while the rest of the word is deleted:

The children wanted to b_____ a treehouse. They wanted to have one big enough for six p_____ . They were looking for a good pl_____ to put it. They looked for a sh_____ tree with lots of br_____ . They picked the oak tree in John's y_____ . It took them six days to f_____ the treehouse.

For children who do not yet have much reading vocabulary, the above procedure can be used with single sentences using known vocabulary except for the word with only the first or first two letters given.

For a child who may seem not to use context clues in reading, a teacher may find it advisable to use some oral context activities and then follow the oral activities with simple written examples. For example, the teacher might ask a child to supply a missing word while listening to statements such as these.

"It is so hot, I'd like to go for a swim in the _____. How would you finish what I said? Yes, you could say *lake* or *pool* or *ocean*. All of those words would make sense."

"I would like to go for a ride on a _____. How can you finish what I said? Yes, you could say *airplane*. Could you say anything else? Good, a *bus*. Anything else? Right, *horse*. How about a *sailboat* or a *train*?"

"The children had a _____ for a pet."

In the three preceding examples more than one response was possible and should be encouraged. Some children need considerable practice to acquire the flexibility to suggest alternative possibilities. In reading, some children become overly concerned about having "*the* right answer."

Context clues in word attack refer to the use of surrounding reading material to determine the meaning and pronunciation of an unfamiliar word. Effective use of context is dependent upon the syntactical patterns of language to derive meaning from print. Isolated word study deprives the reader of syntactical and semantic clues found in larger units of language. Because the language experience approach works with meaningful materials in sentence and story contexts, the use of context clues can be easily taught and applied. As children first learn to read their spoken language, the use of context reading is evident. When a child does not know a word while reading a sentence, the teacher may say, "If you remember the rest of what you read you may be able to figure out the word."

Contextual closure exercises that omit one word from a sentence can be developed with material from language experience stories. For example, a teacher may take sentences from a group experience story, write them on the board, on a transparency for the overhead projector, or on another chart. She can then ask the children if they can select from the words written on word cards or on the board the word that belongs in a particular sentence. Closure activities can be done in the same manner with individual stories with words from word banks. Small groups can be formed with children reading sentences from their individual stories, leaving out a word, and asking the group members to suggest appropriate words. Such an activity helps to teach the concept of synonyms and can extend both the speaking and reading vocabularies. The use of context clues is also combined with phonic and structural clues in attacking unfamiliar words.

DICTIONARY

Functional and informal dictionary activities can be included in the language experience framework. The interest in word study, which was a theme of chapter 5, should encourage children to be enthusiastic about using dictionaries. As children read and write independently, they should be encouraged to use the dictionary as an aid to meaning, spelling, and pronunciation. At every grade level in the elementary school, dictionaries should always be available for reference in the classroom writing center and reading corner. A number of easy, attractively-illustrated picture dictionaries are now available for beginning readers. Beyond the primary levels, other commercial dictionaries can be provided.

All of the word bank experiences with alphabetizing and word meaning should encourage dictionary study. Word banks can lead to the development of class and individual dictionaries as children compile definitions and alphabetize and list words in dictionary form in a notebook. The concept of multiple meanings can be developed through discussion of the words in word banks, and children can compose a group bank of "Words with More than One Meaning."

Alphabetizing in functional situations with language experience activities can be included in the total program. For example, in one primary class the children made a class dictionary of names, addresses, and telephone numbers. The original purpose was to have a list for sending Christmas and Valentine cards. The teacher explained that directories are alphabetized according to the last name. Children can also compile glossaries or dictionaries to accompany some of the group books. The games and activities listed in the pamphlet *Fun with Words*[7] and the activities suggested at the beginning of the *Junior* and *Beginning Thorndike-Barnhart Dictionaries* (Scott, Foresman and Co.) can make the teaching of dictionary skills lively and interesting.

Recording Children's Learning

In chart 1, an overview of the content of phonics and structural analysis is shown in a form that can be used for recording a child's progress. Prereading content of letter name knowledge, visual discrimination, and auditory discrimination is included. Space is provided for recording when a skill is taught and when it is mastered. The checklist is written with descriptions of the child's behavior which would demonstrate competency. For more complete discussions of word analysis content and instruction, see the suggested readings at the end of the chapter.

CHART 1
Word Analysis Checklist

Child _____

Prereading*

Can auditorily discriminate between likenesses and differences in beginning sounds

Taught   Mastered

_____   _____

---

*See chapter 8 for a discussion of prereading. The content listed here is only a small part of a prereading program.

Can auditorily discriminate by recognizing rhyming words

Taught   Mastered

_____   _____

Can identify letter forms by name

Taught   Mastered

_____   _____

Can visually discriminate by matching capital letter forms*

Taught   Mastered

_____   _____

Can visually discriminate by matching lowercase letter forms*

Taught   Mastered

_____   _____

Can visually discriminate by matching word forms*

Taught   Mastered

_____   _____

Consonants

Single Consonants: b, hard c, soft c, d, f, hard g, soft g, h, j, k, l, m, n, p, qu, r, s, t, v, w, x, y, z

Can identify in initial position in words

Taught   Mastered

_____   _____

Can identify in medial position in words

Taught   Mastered

_____   _____

Can identify in final position in words

Taught   Mastered

_____   _____

_____

*Both simultaneous and successive discrimination should be included. (see p. 103).

123

Can substitute consonants to attack new words

    in initial position (Jack to back)

        Taught   Mastered

        —————   —————

    in final position (bed to beg)

        Taught   Mastered

        —————   —————

Consonant blends or clusters: *l* blends: bl, cl, fl, gl, pl, sl, spl
                                  r blends: br, cr, dr, fr, gr, pr, tr, scr, spr, str, thr
                                  s blends: sc, sk, sl, sm, sn, sp, st, sw, str

Can identify *l* blends in spoken and written words

        Taught   Mastered

        —————   —————

Can identify *r* blends in spoken and written words

        Taught   Mastered

        —————   —————

Can identify *s* blends in spoken and written words

        Taught   Mastered

        —————   —————

Can substitute blends to attack new words

        Taught   Mastered

        —————   —————

Consonant Digraphs: sh, ch, wh, th (both voiced and unvoiced)

Can identify in spoken and written words

        Taught   Mastered

        —————   —————

Can substitute digraphs to attack new words

        Taught   Mastered

        —————   —————

Vowels

Long, short, r-controlled sounds

Can recognize long vowel sounds in spoken and written words

Taught   Mastered

_____   _____

Can recognize short vowel sounds in spoken and written words

Taught   Mastered

_____   _____

Can recognize *r*-controled vowel sounds in spoken and written words

Taught   Mastered

_____   _____

Other vowel sounds: long oo, short oo, oi and oy diphthong, ou and ow diphthong, y as long i and long e.*

Can recognize long and short *oo* in spoken and written words

Taught   Mastered

_____   _____

Can recognize *oi* and *oy* diphthongs in spoken and written words

Taught   Mastered

_____   _____

Can recognize *y* as long i and long e in spoken and written words

Taught   Mastered

_____   _____

Vowel generalizations: The generalizations which apply to these key words (1) gō, (2) gĕt, (3) rāĭn, (4) rīdé*

Can state and apply generalization No. 1.

Taught   Mastered

_____   _____

_____

*Value of this content can be questioned.

125

Can state and apply generalization No. 2.

Taught   Mastered

_____   _____

Can state and apply generalization No. 3.

Taught   Mastered

_____   _____

Can state and apply generalization No. 4.

Taught   Mastered

_____   _____

Syllabication*

Generalizations: 1. vccv   2. vcv   3. c + le = last syllable
                lad/der   lā/dy   lā/dle

Can state and apply generalization No. 1.

Taught   Mastered

_____   _____

Can state and apply generalization No. 2.

Taught   Mastered

_____   _____

Can state and apply generalization No. 3.

Taught   Mastered

_____   _____

Can apply vowel generalizations to determine vowel sounds in syllables.

Taught   Mastered

_____   _____

---

*The value of teaching syllabication is questionable according to some authorities (See Suggested Readings).

Structural Analysis

Compound words, contractions, roots, prefixes, and suffixes

Can recognize and attack compound words

Taught   Mastered

_____   _____

Can recognize and attack contractions

Taught   Mastered

_____   _____

Can recognize and attack words with roots, prefixes, and suffixes

Taught   Mastered

_____   _____

Structural Changes: (1) Drop silent *e* (ride to riding) (2) double consonant (hop to hopping) (3) *y* to *i* (candy to candies)

Can read and spell words following generalization No. 1.

Taught   Mastered

_____   _____

Can read spell words following generalization No. 2.

Taught   Mastered

_____   _____

Can read and spell words following generalization No. 3.

Taught   Mastered

_____   _____

Meaning Cues

Can use context clues to acquire new reading vocabulary.

Taught   Mastered

_____   _____

127

Another kind of record, which can be useful for teachers, would be similar to chart 2. This record can be kept as certain content is stressed with a notation of which content has been taught to and mastered by individuals.

CHART 2

STUDENT	INITIAL CONSONANTS
	b c d f g h j k l m n p qu r s t v w y z
Ann	x x x x x x x x x x x x x x x x x x x x x
Sue	x x x x x x x x x x x x x x x x x x x x x
Bob	x x x x x x
Kathy	x x / / / / /
David	/ / / / / / /

/ = taught   x = mastered

At a glance, it is possible to tell which skills have been introduced to and mastered by individuals. For example, as recorded on chart 2. Ann and Sue have mastered all of the phoneme-grapheme relationships for consonants in the initial position in words. By studying the same chart, one finds that David has not mastered the content to which he has been exposed. Such records can be helpful as a record of instruction and for noting progress, as a basis for forming skill groups, and as a source of information for conferences with parents.

SUMMARY

Effective teaching of reading must include the development of strategies for independent word analysis. Many functional situations in the language experience approach may be used to illustrate or to reinforce specific strategies. Instruction in using meaning cues, structural or morphemic analysis, and phonics can strengthen children's ability to deal with unfamiliar printed words.

Notes

1. MaryAnne Hall, *The Language Experience Approach for Teaching Reading: A Research Perspective* (Newark, Del.: International Reading Association and ERIC/RCS, 1978), pp. 10–11.
2. Dan M. Baxley, "The Utility of Forty-five Phonic Generalizations as Applied to Oral Vocabularies of Economically Limited Spanish Surname Children," Doctoral Dissertation, Arizona State University, 1972.
3. Mary Ann Dzama, "A Comparative Study of Natural vs. Frequency Control Vocabularies on the Basis of Forty-five Phonic Generalizations," Doctoral Dissertation, University of Virginia, 1972.
4. MaryAnne Hall, Jerilyn K. Ribovich, and Christopher J. Ramig, *Reading and the Elementary School Child* (New York: Van Nostrand, 1979), pp. 122–23.
5. Morton Botel, *How to Teach Reading*, 4th ed. (Chicago: Follett, 1968), pp. 64–65.
6. Hall, Ribovich, and Raming, *Reading and the Elementary School Child*, pp. 122–123.
7. *Fun with Words* (Glenview, Ill.: Scott, Foresman and Company, 1962).

Suggested Readings

BOTEL, MORTON. *How To Teach Reading*, 4th ed. Chicago: Follett, 1968. Step-by-step teaching procedures are outlined with specific examples. A brief overview is given of the content of word analysis.

GROFF, PATRICK. "Fifteen Flaws of Phonics," *Elementary English* 50 (January 1972): 35–40. Groff's article requires that a teacher reexamine beliefs about the teaching of phonics.

HALL, MARYANNE; RIBOVICH, JERILYN K; RAMIG, CHRISTOPHER J. *Reading and the Elementary School Child.* New York: Van Nostrand, 1979. Word analysis and its place in a total reading program are included in chapters 4, 5, and 6. Both content and instructional procedures are featured.

SMITH, FRANK. *Understanding Reading.* New York: Holt, Rinehart and Winston, 1979. This probing psycholinguistic analysis of the reading process raises many questions about how reading is learned and about which language cues are helpful to a reader.

WILSON, ROBERT M., and HALL, MARYANNE, *Programmed Word Attack for Teachers*, 3rd ed. Columbus: Charles E. Merrill, 1979. For the teacher unfamiliar with the content of word attack, this programmed text provides a comprehensive overview.

ZUCK, L. V. "Some Questions about the Teaching of Syllabication Rules," *The Reading Teacher* 27 (March 1974): 583–88. Zuck presents the argument that teaching of syllabication is not useful.

10

THE LANGUAGE EXPERIENCE CLASSROOM

Reading as a language experience has been described, and the instructional dimensions have been explored in the preceding chapters. Now, certain overall concerns of the teacher who wishes to employ this approach are examined. What is the classroom environment like? How is the language experience classroom organized? How is learning evaluated in this approach?

THE TEACHER

The most important single influence on learning in any given classroom is the teacher. Attitudes, rapport with children, arrangement of stimuli for learning, and knowledge and skill are hard to measure objectively but are extremely influential in the teacher's effectiveness.

Teachers' expectations of children's performance affect learning. Language experience teachers must believe that children can learn through personal involvement in situations requiring communication and that children's ability to use language effectively can be developed through the use of their language as the base of teaching and learning.

The teacher's interpretation of reading and the processes of learning and teaching in relation to the individual influences the effectiveness of her teaching. In this approach, the teacher *must* encourage freedom of expression in a setting in which creativity can flourish in order to promote growth in the ability to communicate.

Attitudes

Essential attitudes of the teacher in the language experience framework of teaching reading are

1. acceptance of each child's language *as it is,* not as the teacher wishes it to be,
2. recognition of the creative nature of this approach,
3. recognition of reading as a language activity that serves as a communication tool and integration of the teaching of reading and language.

Acceptance of child's speech

In all language activities the teacher must accept the child's language as it is; the teacher must not convey rejection by altering the language in order to have grammatically correct sentences. Allen states, ". . . it is important to remember that each child has a natural language and that new language learnings must be related to it, faulty as it may be."[1] In their concern for developing language facility, teachers must be careful not to reject a child's existing level of communication. Language development will be fostered by opportunities for communicating personally valued ideas, not by a program of intensive correction. In the early stages, correction of speech may serve to block oral and written expression rather than to encourage them. Lefevre warns:

> If teachers insist on instant correction, incessant correction, of every
> so-called mistake the child makes in speech, reading, and writing,
> the child will close up like an oyster. He will hate to recite and hate
> to write in school.[2]

Every child exhibits many deviations (yet linguistically plausible ones) from adult norms in learning to talk, but with opportunity, experience, and encouragement, he develops the ability to communicate through speech. The process of communication is more important than the correctness of the mechanics. The preceding statements should not imply that children be encouraged to learn incorrect speech patterns; instead, the first concern in the early stages of instruction is to develop the understanding that thoughts can be communicated orally and encoded with written symbols which then

131

can be read with understanding. The teacher does have a responsibility to provide appropriate language models and opportunities for expression so that communication skill does improve.

Creative nature

Acceptance is a key word for the teacher who recognizes the creative nature of the language experience approach. An attitude and climate of acceptance must be present if creativity is to flourish. Wilt comments on the importance of accepting a child's creative effort:

> The teacher should accept enthusiastically and generously whatever personal expression the child dreams up. Regardless of the creative result, he must always realize that the process is of far more consequence than the product.[3]

The language experience teacher will need to believe sincerely that children can be creative if teachers permit that creativity to be expressed and if they seek to reach it in a variety of ways. Teachers must believe in and develop pupil authorship.

Integrated process

Much has been stated in the preceding material concerning the stress on the interrelatedness of language and reading in the language experience approach. Acknowledgment of this concept is so important, however, that this third basic attitude of the teacher of recognition that reading and language should be taught as an integrated process is stressed again. The teacher has the responsibility for presenting situations that stimulate ever-increasing facility with language. The chasm that has often existed in elementary schools between the teaching of language and the teaching of reading is bridged in the language experience approach. Reading is viewed, not as a separate subject, but as a part of the language program. As children learn to communicate more effectively orally, they are learning to communicate more effectively through reading.

Classroom Organization

In facilitating instruction in the language experience approach, whole group, small group, and individual learning situations are utilized. While individualization of instruction is a prime consideration, group instruction is desirable for certain experiences and, in many cases, is more efficient than individual instruction. However, the individual nature of the approach is one of its major attributes and individual response constantly encouraged. Large group experiences can often lead to different individual activities for each child as he creates his personal reading materials.

Large Group Instruction

Literature experiences, group experience stories, planning sessions, and creative writing can occur with a total class group. Group interaction through discussion is valuable since in this way children learn to be careful listeners, to respect and respond to the ideas of others, and to express their ideas in ways to be understood by others. Certain language activities involving word banks can also be used with large groups.

Small Group Instruction

Small group instruction is desirable for the sharing of personal writing, for instruction in specified strategies, and for directed instruction in reading for those pupils with the same reading level or those who are working on the same concept or strategy. Small groups can be temporary and disbanded when no longer needed. Pupils can work together in small groups without teacher direction as they share writing, talk about words, and discuss their independent reading.

Children working in pairs or teams can read to each other, work together in building sentences with the word banks, and share their individual stories. Small groups can be formed on an interest basis as children who have written or have read materials on a particular topic share their information. Projects on which several children work together provide another situation for small group instruction.

Individual Instruction

Individual instruction is offered when a teacher records a child's personal story and when selected rereading activities are conducted with the story. (See p. 38). Using the individualized reading approach in conjunction with the language experience approach is favored by many teachers. The individual pupil-teacher conference is used in both the individualized and language experience approaches to instruction. In the conference situation the teacher observes a child's reading needs, suggests material for future reading, and provides needed skill instruction.

Learning Centers

When organizing a language experience instructional program, the teacher should look at the total language program, not just at the reading program. The language experience activities described in this book rest upon a philosophy of integration of all the language arts. The language experience class-

133

room should provide ideas and materials for worthwhile independent activities in the language arts. Teachers are concerned about the time needed for language experience instruction. Classroom organization that uses language experience activities for independent learning adds considerably to the effectiveness of the approach and to the efficient use of time since much learning can occur in the self-directed activities. Learning centers that offer planned reinforcement of specific learning and through which children can pursue individual interests are featured in increasing numbers in today's classrooms. Additional experiences with a particular skill or topic can be done independently in the centers. They offer activities that are not required or standardized for all children but which serve as an opportunity for encouraging and extending pupil interests. Learning centers of particular importance in the implementation of the language experience approach are a reading center, a listening center, a writing center, a discussion center, an art center, and a bookbinding center.

Learning centers offer language experience activities for independent study.

Reading center

The reading center should foster wide independent reading as materials of a variety of types and levels are available to students. The center should be an inviting place with attractive displays and comfortable chairs or rugs. The children's literature in the center will lead to creative writing and other language experience activities. Pupil displays of art work and writing correlated with literature should be evident here. The reading center, too, is a place for displaying children's independent writing in the form of individual and class books. Children should participate in the arrangement of the center and can assume partial responsibility for the displays of their work. Many of the ideas suggested in chapters 3, 4, and 6 can be used in the reading center.

Listening center

A listening center should include a tape recorder, record player, sets of headphones, and plug-in jacks. Teachers have found that tapes and records, which can be used by children with little or no teacher direction, can be extremely useful both for direct instruction and independent learning. Children's literature selections can be taped and replayed by individuals or small groups. Children can record their creative stories. Motivation for meaningful oral reading can be provided as pupils tape materials for their classmates and for other classes and grades. As children find enjoyable passages in their independent reading, they can tape these. Teachers can play the tapes to evaluate pupils' oral reading.

For directed lessons with listening center materials, teachers can tape directions to correlate with a particular lesson and can have children follow directions from the tape without requiring the presence of the teacher. Certain phonics lessons are quite appropriate for taped presentation. Publishers now have a quantity of tapes and records to correlate with all content areas. Also popular for these centers are "read-along" materials which include books so children can watch the print while hearing the story on the tape. Many teachers are making their own "read-along" materials using favorite literature selections and pupil-composed language experience stories.

Writing center

Another important center is the writing center, which should stimulate personal writing and additional independent activities directly correlated with the language experience instruction. The writing center should include such essentials as commercial and class picture dictionaries, class word banks, pencils, crayons, and paper. Pictures and objects can be placed in this center to stimulate creative writing. As in all centers, ideas will need to be changed frequently to maintain interest. The materials in the writing center can provide an excellent means for following up previous lessons or activities. For example, if a class is studying descriptive words, the teacher can reinforce this content by asking the children to write descriptive words for objects or pictures in the writing center or to write a story using descriptive words. The writing center should serve as an invitation to write, not as a required assignment for pupils.

Of course, at the very early stages of reading development, the activities in the center may need considerable structure, but as children improve in reading, less help will be necessary. Beginning readers may wish to practice handwriting by copying a group experience story, but they should not be required to do this. In the very early stage of learning to read, model sentences can be used in the writing center with some element of word choice. For example, to provide practice in reading and writing color words, objects and pictures along with word cards for each object and picture can be placed in the writing center. The model sentence could be "A _____ is yellow," with pictures of pencils, paper, bananas, pears, the sun, and butter. Other model sentence ideas might be "Round things" or "I like to _____," with pictures and phrases such as "ride my bike," "play football," "play with dolls," or "run in the leaves." Children could write a sentence, illustrate it, and use it for a group book.

In chapter 4, teaching written expression is discussed. A teacher can follow up the types and techniques of writing with examples in the writing center. For example, if a class were working on tall tales, the writing

135

center could feature examples from both children's writings and literature. Pictures or topics for additional tall tales could be suggested as an independent activity. This use of the writing center could be adapted for each type and technique of writing.

A popular idea for a writing center is the use of pictures with questions and captions to stimulate writing. Some suggestions are

1. Can you write an animal story?
2. Can you write an imaginary story?
3. Can you write a story about snow?
4. Can you make up a surprise ending for these pictures?
5. What descriptive words describe how the child felt in this picture?

Related to a writing center or as separate centers could be a newspaper center and an editing center. In the newspaper center, students assume roles of reporters, columnists, editor, and copy editor. In the editing center, children submit their writing for suggestions from other students.

The ideas for the writing center are inexhaustible since the illustrations, captions, and questions can be extremely varied. Often pupil-teacher conferences and group sharing sessions will occur after students have developed a draft based on an idea suggested in the center.

DISCUSSION CENTER

Stimuli for language experience stories can be placed in the discussion center for small groups to gather and discuss their ideas prior to writing and/or dictating stories. Open-ended questions and situations can serve to stimulate creative and critical thinking. Examples of questions are "What do you think about . . .?" "What would you do if . . .?" Appointing pupil leaders to conduct some discussions may lead to more involvement in oral language than when the teacher always serves as a leader. The center may make it possible for a teacher to offer additional oral situations for some children who are minimally involved in large group discussions for stories.

ART CENTER

Some teachers may not regard the art center as a part of the reading environment. However, in language experience reading programs, art is an invaluable stimulus for creating through language. Art activities often lead to language involvement, and language activities often lead to artistic expression. The products which contain illustrations are usually far more appealing than those which do not, and the illustrations contribute to the pride in authorship which is so important in language experience learning. Literature experiences lead easily to interpretation through art. The displays recommended for the reading center offer an excellent way to incorporate art with the reading program.

Bookbinding CENTER

A helpful center in language experience classrooms is a bookbinding center that makes it possible for children to make attractive and durable products from their stories. Needed are cloth for covers, heavy cardboard, large needles, and thread. The booklet *Cover to Cover*[4] provides detailed, illustrated explanations of the steps in bookbinding. The following material is reprinted from *Cover to Cover*.*

Step 1
Stack the completed pages and add two extra pages, one before the title page and one after the final page.

Step 2
Fasten the pages together along the left edge or at the top, depending on the way the book is to open. Staples will be adequate for books of a few pages, but sewing is more durable. Sewing may be done by hand and can be done on a sewing machine using the longest stitch.

Step 3
Cut two pieces of cardboard one-fourth inch larger in each direction than the page size. If shirt cardboard is used, a double thickness may be desired.

Step 4
Tape the two pieces of cardboard together with a one-fourth inch separation between them so that the cover is hinged.

* Reprinted by permission.

137

Step 5
Place the cardboard on the cover material and cut a piece large enough to extend one full inch around the outer edge of the cardboard.

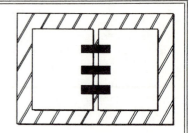

Step 6
Remove the carboard and coat the reverse side of the cover material with glue. An easy formula is 3 parts Elmer's Glue and one part water. This can be spread easily. Replace the hinged cardboard and fold the edges of the cover material around the cardboard. Pull the cover edges tightly to remove puckers and bubbles.

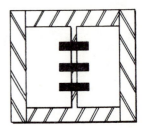

Step 7
Cut a piece of colored construction paper large enough to cover the inside of the book cover and paste it in place over the edge of the cover material.

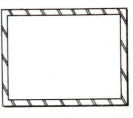

Step 8
Fasten the bound pages into the book with tape. Construction paper the same color as the inside of the cover can be cut and pasted in place to cover the tape.

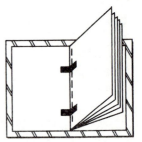

Evaluation

Evaluation is a continuous process and a part of all curriculum experiences. Informal evaluation will occur in everyday situations with spoken and written language. More formal evaluation will come in the form of record keeping and standardized testing. Specific suggestions for record keeping are presented by Braun for those teachers who wish to have very systematic records.[5]

The observant teacher can examine children's performance and reactions to note individual progress and needs. The commonly accepted belief that evaluation of student progress in language experience programs is too dependent on teacher observation and judgment is refuted by Froese. He cites research that indicates teacher Judgment does correspond with general test results.[6] Dixon suggests that language experience stories are useful "diagnostic-evaluative tools worth further consideration."[7] For those teachers (and administrators) who are concerned about the achievement of students in language experience programs, the International Reading Association publication *The Language Experience Approach to Reading Instruction: A Research Perspective* gives extensive documentation that these programs are effective.[8]

The checklists suggested in chapter 9 are also part of the evaluation. Self evaluation is encouraged as children note the increase in vocabulary in their word banks for both reading and spelling, as they keep folders of their written stories, as they keep records of the books chosen and read individually, and as they discuss their progress with the teacher. The pride in authorship should lead to positive evaluation. Stauffer relates an incident at the end of a school year of a first grade child rereading the stories composed in November. The child's comment was, "That's the way I wrote when I was little."[9]

In the language experience approach, the teacher must evaluate children's learning in reading and the other language arts in terms of the instructional goals discussed in chapter 2. Those goals can be stated in question form as guides for teacher evaluation of reading and language programs: Are children growing in their ability to use reading as a medium of communication? Are their reading vocabularies increasing? Are they developing favorable attitudes and genuine interest in reading? Are they using effective strategies to unlock unfamiliar words? Questions related to communication through language should also be asked in regard to the goal statements of Smith[10] and Applegate[11] found in chapter 2. The teacher should ask, too, whether children are responding creatively in the language experience activities.

The following checklist may facilitate evaluation of the implementation of language experience programs.

Checklist for Observing the Implementation
of a Language Experience Program

I. Teacher accepts children's spoken language.
   a. The teacher writes children's language in the forms they have used. Standard spelling is used, but the children's syntax and vocabulary is used unless a child suggests a change or correction.
   b. The teacher accepts children's spoken language as a valid communication system in classroom activities.

139

II. Teacher uses child-produced materials for teaching reading.
   a. The teacher uses group experience stories for subgroups (can be flexible and temporary, formed on basis of interest—not merely achievement) for direct instruction. (1–2 per week per group)
   b. The teacher uses individual experience stories as part of the direct instructional program. (1–2 per week per individual)
   c. The teacher uses group books as part of the direct instructional program. (1–2 per week)
   d. The teacher uses individual word banks as part of the direct instructional program. (See III.)
   e. The teacher gives children copies of their language experience products, and these copies are both used for directed instruction and for independent activities.
   f. The teacher uses the child-produced materials for direct instruction in comprehension, vocabulary, and word analysis.
   g. The teacher encourages interest in learning to read through children's feelings of success, motivation, and pride in authorship.

III. Teacher uses word banks as part of the reading instruction.
   a. The teacher gives children the words they select and can identify independently in their language experience products for their word banks.
   b. The teacher uses the word banks for direct instruction in vocabulary activities. (Ex: Matching cards to story context, building sentences, classification activities)

IV. Teacher integrates reading with other language arts.
   a. The teacher develops reading material from communication situations in which listening and speaking are stressed. (See V.)
   b. The teacher incorporates opportunities for interpretive response through discussion, drama, art, and writing.
   c. The teacher encourages independent writing (to accompany art work, use of writing center, instruction with written expression).
   d. The teacher shows the relationship between spoken and written language as she writes children's dictation and reads the dictated material to them.
   e. The teacher points out in *meaningful situations* some of the mechanics of written language. (Ex: "This is the end of David's idea. What mark do you see?" or "This is the beginning of Sandra's idea. What kind of letter do you see?")

V. Teacher provides a rich oral language program. (Also see IV–b.)
   a. The teacher reads children's literature to students every day.
   b. The teacher encourages discussion about literature, children's interests, classroom events, and other appropriate concerns.
   c. The teacher encourages discussion before pupils dictate or write their experience materials.

VI. Teacher emphasizes reading comprehension.
   a. The teacher stresses meaning regardless of reading level.
   b. The teacher seeks to constantly extend concepts and vocabulary.

c. The teacher shows questioning strategies which promote creative, evaluative, and divergent experiences.

d. The teacher incorporates opportunities for interpretive responses through discussing drama, art, and writing. (Same as IV–b.)

e. The teacher uses literature models and children's writing to develop understanding of passage structure and sense of story.

VII. Teacher displays children's language experience products.

a. Children's written language products are displayed attractively on bulletin boards and are read voluntarily by children as an independent activity.

b. Children's personally produced books (both individual and group) are displayed in a classroom library/reading center and are read voluntarily by children as an independent activity.

c. Large group experience charts are displayed prominently in the classroom. These charts are used for directed and independent follow-up activities.

VIII. Teacher uses centers to promote independent learning.

a. The teacher provides an attractive writing center (with stimuli for writing, necessary materials, group word banks, picture dictionaries).

b. Reading (literature) center, art center, listening center, discussion center, and bookbinding center are present.

Final Summary

Teaching reading as a language experience rests on a philosophy of personal, communicative, creative, and functional learning and teaching. Instruction is built on children's existing level of language expression as speech is encoded with written symbols and as they read the written record of their spoken thoughts.

Language study in speaking, listening, reading, and writing occurs in situations which contain and stimulate a high degree of pupil involvement. Pupil-developed materials are central to teaching in this framework. The language experience approach is used as a bridge from prereading to beginning reading as a component of a balanced reading program with other approaches, as a means of reaching the discouraged remedial reader and the adult illiterate, and as a means of providing materials relevant to children not of the mainstream culture.

The instructional program stresses written expression, vocabulary development, and literary experiences in a classroom based on flexibility, receptiveness, and stimulation. The classroom setting includes learning centers where children can pursue independent language activities. Individual, small group, and total group instruction are included in the language experiences. As teachers evaluate the children's ability to communicate through spoken and written language, they base their evaluation on the goals of reading and language instruction.

141

Notes

1. Roach Van Allen, *Attitudes and the Art of Teaching Reading* (Washington, D.C.: National Educational Association, 1965), p. 6.

2. Carl A. Lefevre, "Language and Self; Fulfillment of Trauma? Part I," *Elementary English* 43 (February 1966): 127.

3. Miriam E. Wilt, *Creativity in the Elementary School* (New York: Appleton-Century-Crofts, 1959), p. 8.

4. *Cover to Cover* (Chicago: Encyclopaedia Britannica Press). This is a free booklet.

5. Carl Braun, "Recordkeeping," in *An Experience-Based Approach to Language and Reading*, eds. Carl Braun and Victor Froese (Baltimore: University Park Press, 1977), pp. 223–233.

6. Victor Froese, "To Talk of Many Things," in *An Experience-Based Approach to Language and Reading*, eds. Carl Braun and Victor Froese (Baltimore: University Park Press, 1977), pp. 211–222.

7. Carol N. Dixon, "Language Experience Stories as a Diagnostic Tool," *Language Arts* 54 (May 1977): 501–505.

8. MaryAnne Hall, *The Language Experience Approach to Reading Instruction: A Research Perspective* (Newark, Del.: International Reading Association and ERIC/RCS, 1978).

9. Russell G. Stauffer, *The Language Experience Approach to the Teaching of Reading* (New York: Harper and Row, 1970), p. 107.

10. James A. Smith, *Adventures in Communication* (Boston: Allyn and Bacon, 1972), pp. 91–93.

11. Mauree Applegate, *Easy in English* (Evanston, Ill.: Row, Peterson and Company, 1960), p. 8.

Suggested Readings

ALLEN, ROACH VAN. *Language Experiences in Reading.* Chicago: Encyclopedia Britannica Press, 1974. In the manuals for language experience programs in these materials, Allen describes the use of centers as part of the ongoing language experience classroom.

BRAUN, CARL, and FROESE, VICTOR, eds. *An Experience-Based Approach to Language and Reading.* Baltimore: University Park Press, 1977. Braun and Froese include evaluation as one of the major sections of their book, and chapters 11 and 12 give specific suggestions for evaluating both students' learning and the instructional program.

DIXON, CAROL N. "Language Experience Stories as a Diagnostic Tool," *Language Arts* 54 (May 1977): 501–505. Dixon presents a checklist to be used for diagnosis with language experience stories for kindergarten and first grade students.

WAYANT, LOUISE F., and WILSON, ROBERT M. *Learning Centers . . . A Guide for Effective Use.* Paoli, Pa.: The Instructo Corporation, 1974. Teachers who wish specific guidelines for implementing learning centers will find this reference particularly helpful.

Index

143

145